Instruments in the Redeemer's Hands

How to Help Others Change

STUDY GUIDE

Paul David Tripp
Timothy S. Lane, Contributor

New Growth Press

WWW.NEWGROWTHPRESS.COM

Instruments in the Redeemer's Hands: How to Help Others Change
Study Guide

New Growth Press, Greensboro, NC 27404
Copyright © 2000 by Christian Counseling & Educational Foundation
Copyright © 2005, 2010 by New Growth Press
Published in 2005 as *Helping Others Change*

Cover Design: faceoutbooks, Nate Salciccioli and Jeff Miller, www.faceoutbooks.com

Typesetting: Lisa Parnell, lparnell.com

ISBN-13: 978-1-935273-04-2
ISBN-10: 1-935273-04-3

Printed in the United States of America

24 23 22 21 20 19 18 17   12 13 14 15 16

A Word of Welcome

Welcome to *Instruments in the Redeemer's Hands*. We are thankful for you and your desire to be effective for Christ. Our prayer is that this course will produce a wonderful harvest of lasting change in you and in those you reach.

Perhaps a few words would be helpful about the course you are about to take.

1. Our goal in this course is to equip you for personal growth and ministry. What is here has been carefully and prayerfully included and tested in churches throughout the country.

2. We use the word *counseling* throughout this course, but by no means do we limit its definition to the more formal, professional meaning. When the course talks about *counseling*, it means "personal ministry." It's talking about getting alongside people to serve them — to assist them in making the changes God wants them to make. This kind of counseling is not only a formal ministry of the church; it's meant to be the lifestyle of every believer. The principles of this course should be lived out in the hallways, family rooms, and minivans of everyday life.

3. As you experience God changing your heart, you will bring integrity and enthusiasm to personal ministry that cannot be found any other way. Ask God to reveal things to you and to change you as you seek to be his instrument of change.

4. Although this course "systematizes" personal ministry, biblical counseling is much more than a system of change. In reality, the most radical difference between biblical counseling and everything else is the belief that people need more than a system of redemption; they need a redeemer! Our real goal is to encourage you to get to know the Lord so that you:

   - Rest in God's sovereignty
   - Rely on the resources of his grace
   - Practically do his will

This curriculum is intensely Christ-centered because we believe that in him are hidden "all the treasures of wisdom and knowledge" (Colossians 2:3). Look for this emphasis in every lesson.

Let me say again that we are excited that you are embarking on this journey. Remember, we are here to help and support you in any way we can. Our hope is that this course will be just the beginning of a long ministry partnership between CCEF and your church or ministry.

In Christ,

Paul David Tripp
Timothy S. Lane

Acknowledgments

It would be impossible to acknowledge the host of people who have contributed to the content and development of this curriculum over the years. However, I must mention a few. Thanks to Sue Lutz, whose editorial work has made this a much better training tool. Jayne Clark contributed her organizational skill and made a dream a doable project. Karen Barnard typed and retyped draft after draft until the job was done. The faculty of CCEF encouraged and supported me throughout the design and writing of the curriculum, and contributed to its content. The entire staff of CCEF has touched this project in some way. Thanks to all of you.

We want to offer special thanks to all the churches around the country that were willing to test this course. You have encouraged us and sharpened the curriculum. Your work has been a very important step in creating the final product.

Our particular gratitude goes to the churches and individuals who gave sacrificially to support the development of this curriculum. This is the most costly and time-consuming project CCEF has ever done, and we could not have completed it without your help. Your partnership has not only enabled us to continue, but it has encouraged us along the way. On behalf of the churches around the world that will use this material and the myriad of people who will grow and change as a result, we say thank you.

Few things in ministry have so clearly depicted to us what Paul says about the church in Ephesians 4:16: "From him the whole body, joined and held together by every supporting ligament, grows and builds itself up in love, as each part does its work."

Course Outline
Instruments in the Redeemer's Hands

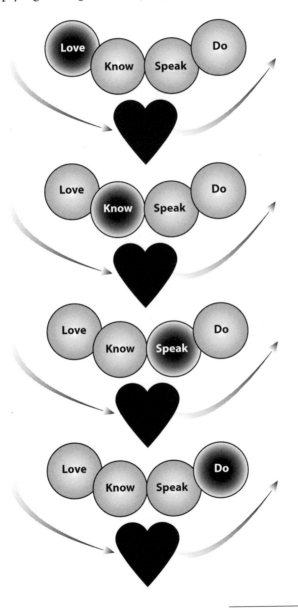

LESSON 1

Do We Really Need Help?

DISCUSS HOMEWORK

INTRODUCTION

Let's first become familiar with your workbooks. As you open them you'll see that there are only a few sections. We'll briefly look at each section so that you can easily find your way.

The first thing to notice is the page at the end of this book that summarizes the course. It is entitled "Instruments in the Redeemer's Hands: At a Glance." We'll be referring to this page often, which is why it is in a place that is easily located. This page gives you a quick preview of the model of growth and ministry that we will be learning: Love-Know-Speak-Do. We will explore in depth these four main elements. The numbers in the diagram indicate the lesson that covers the topic. "Course Outline" in the front of the book lists each lesson that we'll cover in this course. Next, turn to "Word of Welcome" at the beginning of the workbook. Take some time later to read this on your own.

We will spend most of our time in the section entitled "Lesson Content" (p. 3). You will be using these pages to take notes. The intention of those who developed this course is to minimize the amount of notes you need to take. For those who need and are happiest taking more extensive notes, space has been provided.

The last section, "Make It Real," includes your assignments. Yes, that's right, there will be homework—but relax, it won't be collected or graded. This section will help you interact with the content of each lesson so that you can begin to make it a part of your daily life.

This may be the most important section of your workbook because it is the place where you will make the course material your own. You are strongly encouraged to do the assignments so that:

- You will begin to understand the Christian life better (who you are and who you are before God)
- You will begin to think biblically about the issues of living
- You will improve your ministry skills

Now let's begin our first lesson by taking a look at ourselves and remembering an important truth. All of us are both people in need of help and people who have been positioned by God to provide his help to others. We always carry both identities. The one who needs help is struggling with the issues of living and asking important questions. The helper needs to have a firm understanding of the process of biblical change. That is where we will begin in this lesson.

The section below entitled "Concepts and Objectives" is meant to function like a map for each lesson. It will give you a sense of where we're going. Perhaps you've noticed that this section is divided into three parts. *Concepts* lists the truths from this lesson that you need to know and remember. *Personalized* summarizes how those truths need to be applied to your own life. And *Related to Others* points to how each truth sets the agenda for your relationships and for ministry. The initials of these three parts, *CPR,* give us a way of remembering that we are focusing on heart change. By "changing hearts," God is "changing lives"—your own and those you serve.

CONCEPTS AND OBJECTIVES

Concept: Our need for help is not the result of the Fall but the result of being human.

Personalized: I need truth from outside myself to make sense out of life.

Related to others: I need to learn how to be one of God's instruments of change in the lives of others.

LESSON CONTENT

We all come across situations in our own lives or in ministry where we don't know what to do or say. It is in these moments that we are confronted with the reality that God hasn't given us a neat system of change that our own wisdom can figure out. Our hope for ourselves and for others can only be found in the presence and work of Jesus the Redeemer. Both the helper and the person in need depend on his wisdom and his power for change.

A Firm Foundation

As we think about our own growth and about serving as God's instruments of change, we must build a firm biblical foundation for understanding people, their need for help, and how change takes place.

If you were asked to write down a distinctly biblical definition of *discipleship* or *personal ministry,* what would you write?

Our culture tends to view personal change as something that requires the help of a professional. But the Bible has a much fuller and more hopeful perspective. The Bible teaches that personal transformation takes place as our hearts are changed and our minds are renewed by the Holy Spirit. And the two instruments that the Holy Spirit uses are the Word of God and the people of God.

✴ Turn to Isaiah 55:10–13. This is a beautiful word picture of God's plan to bless us and glorify himself through the changes his Word accomplishes in us. In fact, those changes are a sign of his covenant relationship with us (v. 13).

✴ Turn next to Ephesians 4:11–16. Here we see that God has given us one another to help us grow to spiritual maturity. Think of all the intricate interdependencies implied by the image of the church as Christ's body. Both of these passages make it clear that God intends to do a powerful work in us. This means that personal change and growth—including radical change of the deepest kind—can take place:

- When we allow the Holy Spirit to apply God's Word to our hearts
- When we allow God's people to encourage, guide, support, pray for, and challenge us in biblical ways

Few of us have fully tapped the potential for growth and ministry that God has given us with these two resources, but this has been God's plan for us from the beginning. We need a fresh understanding of what the Bible says about this world of personal transformation. We will begin by looking at personal growth and ministry from the vantage point of creation, the Fall, and redemption.

Our Need as Seen in Creation

Follow along with me as I read Genesis 1:26–28. Here we see human need in the broadest sense of the term. God knew that even though Adam and Eve were perfect people living in a perfect world in a perfect relationship with God, they could not figure life out on their own. They could not live independent of God's counsel.

God had to explain who they were and what they were to do with their lives and their surroundings. Adam and Eve's need for help was not the result of sin's entrance into the world. They needed God's help because they were human. To be human is to need help outside of oneself in order to understand and live life.

Even before the fall, we needed help outside of ourselves. And God said . . . .

Adam and Eve had this need because there were three things that separated them from the rest of creation:

1. They were created by God to be revelation receivers.
2. They were created by God to be interpreters.
3. They were created by God to be worshippers.

We all are actively interpreting life, and we all share our interpretations with one another. None of us live life based on the facts, but based on our interpretation of the facts. So, to be human is to need truth outside ourselves in order to make sense out of life. The first instance of help was not person-to-person, but the Wonderful Counselor explaining life to the people he made in his own image.

As we interpret life, we are always expressing some sense of identity. We speak to one another out of some sense of purpose and meaning. We are constantly interpreting life out of a sense of who we are and what we are supposed to be doing, and we are always sharing our interpretations with one another. We all interpret. We are all people of influence.

Our Need as Seen in the Fall

Now turn with me to Genesis 3:1–7. Something very dramatic takes place in this passage. For the very first time in human history, we see the entrance of another voice. This new speaker takes the very same set of facts (discussed by God in Genesis 1 and 2) and gives them a very different interpretation.

If Adam and Eve decide to believe the interpretation of this new speaker, it would be stupid to continue to obey God. Notice that our interpretations, our advice giving, are always agenda-setting. If we reject the words of God and follow the words of the serpent, we will not think about God, ourselves, or life in the same way, and we will not continue to do the same things.

What are the principles we can draw out of this passage to develop a biblical understanding of personal growth and ministry?

What we worship determines

- Thoughts, talk, opinions, advice, and relationships are always agenda setting. Even though we may be unaware of it, we daily tell one another what to desire, think, and do.
- Advice is always moral. It always is defining right and wrong, good and bad, true and false, or healthy and unhealthy. Advice always gives our situations and relationships a moral framework.
- We should hunger for the simple days of Genesis 1 when everything people thought, said, and did was based solely on the words of God. We, however, live in a world of much confusion, where literally thousands of voices speak to us at the same time, each interpreting life and each competing for our hearts.
- We need Scripture to cut through the confusion and make sense out of life for us.

Our Need as Seen in Redemption

Many people have asked the question, "Do believers, who are indwelt by the Holy Spirit and have the Word of God, really need personal ministry? Isn't the cry for this a lack of faith in the Spirit and a lack of confidence in the Bible?" The final passage we will look at speaks in a powerful way to this question.

Let's look at Hebrews 3:12–13. This passage is essentially a warning against falling away from the Lord. The falling away is presented as something that is progressive. Notice the steps:

Sinful (subtle patterns of sin I allow in my life)

Unbelieving (subtle excusing of my sin, backing away from the clear words of Scripture)

Turning away (a loss of my spiritual moorings)

Hardened (heart crusted over with the scabs of sin —no longer tender)

Now what you should ask is, "How could this ever happen to a believer?" This passage declares something about us that explains why this scary warning is necessary. It says that sin is deceitful. And guess who it deceives first? Us! We have no problem seeing the sin in others.

This is the theology of the passage: As long as sin still dwells within us, there will be some aspect of spiritual blindness in all of us. Yes, we can see the speck of dust in another's eye while missing the log that is jutting out of our own (Matthew 7:1–5)! The passage is basically saying that all of us need help because until we are at home with the Lord, all of us will suffer from some degree of spiritual blindness. And, unlike physically blind people, spiritually blind people are often blind to their blindness.

So, what the writer of Hebrews says is that we need daily intervention. All of us are in the same place. There are no "haves" and "have nots." Each of us is in need of help and each is called to help, that is, to function daily as one of God's instruments of change in the lives of others.

If this kind of mutual help is going to become a lifestyle, there are two qualities that each of us needs to have. First, we need the courage of honesty. We cannot be afraid of being lovingly honest. We have to love one another enough to break through the walls of spiritual blindness. Second, we need the humility of approachability. We need to be willing to listen and consider when people challenge us with things that alone we would not see. We need to humbly and joyfully embrace the help that God has provided for us.

Three Questions that Everyone Asks

If we live with and care for people, there are three questions that we have probably asked. These three questions form the basis of any system of growth and transformation. They are questions that we must answer in a distinctly biblical way.

1. Why do people do the things they do? To answer this question we need a biblical theology of human motivation. What does the Bible say causes people to think the things they think, to want what they want, or to do the things they do?

2. How does lasting change take place in a person's life? If we see a person doing something that is wrong or destructive, we want to see change take place in his or her life. What does the Bible say leads to such change? We need a biblical theology of change.

   The *How People Change* curriculum addresses these two questions in depth, beginning in lessons 2 and 3.

3. How can I be an instrument of change in the life of another person? To answer this question we need a biblical methodology of change.

These are the questions we will be addressing throughout this course. Our goal is that we will all be changed by God, ready to be his instruments of change wherever and with whomever he places us.

THE BIG QUESTION: Why do you need help?

CPR

Concepts

1. To be human is to need help outside of myself.

2. Influence always carries a moral agenda.

3. Everyone suffers from some degree of spiritual blindness.

Personalized

1. I need to receive truth outside of myself to make sense out of life.

2. I need to humbly examine why I do and say the things I do.

3. I need to recognize sin's deceitfulness and commit myself to being approachable.

Related to others

1. I need to learn how to be one of God's instruments of change in the lives of others.

2. I need to saturate myself with Scripture so that my interpretations and counsel to others are based on God's Word.

3. I need to recognize how I am influencing others in the relationships and situations of daily life.

Make It Real

1. How will the truths of this lesson shape your prayers about ministry opportunities?

2. Tell about a time in your life when you responded not to the facts of a situation but to your interpretation of the facts. Did you realize it at the time?

3. Describe a time when the Lord used a person or the Word of God to reveal your spiritual blindness. What did you learn about your need for such help? If you were helped by a person, what did he or she do to make it a positive or negative experience?

4. What things keep you from being approachable (being helped)? What things keep you from reaching out (helping)? Ask the Lord to help you in these areas and repent where appropriate.

al

LESSON 2

The Heart Is the Target

DISCUSS HOMEWORK

REVIEW

CONCEPTS AND OBJECTIVES

Concept: The heart is active. It shapes and controls our behavior.

Personalized: I must identify what effectively and functionally rules my heart.

Related to others: I must be committed to be an instrument of heart change in the lives of those around me.

LESSON CONTENT

Let's begin by looking at one of the most important word pictures in the New Testament. This word picture is so important because it reveals Christ's perspective on how people function—that is, why they do the things they do. Turn in your Bibles to Luke 6:43–46.

Christ likens the way we function to a tree. If you plant apple seeds and they take root, you don't expect to see peaches or oranges growing. When you are dealing with a plant, you recognize that there is an organic connection between the roots of the plant and the fruit it produces. The same is true with people.

Let's unpack Christ's illustration. In his example, fruit equals behavior. The fruit (behavior) in this passage is speaking. Christ says something very powerful about our words. Our words are literally the heart overflowing. People don't make us say what we say. Situations don't make us say what we say. Our words are shaped and controlled by our hearts. Fruit is what the tree produces, just as our behavior is what our hearts produce. You and I recognize a tree by the kind of fruit it produces.

The second part of the word picture is equally important but not as obvious. In Christ's example, the roots of the tree equal the heart. This is what is underground. It is not as clearly seen or easily understood. The power of Christ's illustration is in the connection it makes between root and fruit. Christ is saying that the tree has the kind of fruit it does because of the kind of roots it has. The application to us is this: we speak and act the way we do because of what is in our hearts. There may be no more important thing we can say about people and how they function.

You may be asking, "What does all of this have to do with personal growth and ministry?" Christ's word picture sets the direction for both. Let me expand and apply the word picture for you.

Pretend that I have an apple tree in my backyard. Each year it buds and grows apples, but when the apples mature, they are dry, wrinkled, brown, and pulpy. After several years I decide that it is silly to have an apple tree and never be able to eat its fruit. So I decide that I must do something to "fix" the tree.

One Saturday afternoon you look out your window to see me carrying branch cutters, a staple gun, a stepladder, and two bushels of Red Delicious apples into my backyard. You watch as I carefully cut off all the bad apples and staple beautiful red apples onto the branches of the tree. You come out and ask me what I am doing, and I say proudly, "I've finally fixed my apple tree!" What are you thinking about me at this point!?

It is clear that if the tree produces bad apples year after year, there is something wrong with the system of this tree, right down to its very roots. I won't solve the problem by stapling apples onto the tree. What will happen to those new apples? They will rot also because they are not attached to the life-giving roots of the tree.

What does this have to do with personal growth and ministry? The problem with much of what we do to produce growth and change in ourselves and others is that it is nothing more than "fruit stapling." It is a "sin is bad so don't do it" view of change that does not examine the heart behind the behavior. Change that does not reach the heart rarely lasts; it is temporary and cosmetic.

Let's explore the way this passage sets the direction for personal growth and ministry by considering the principles that flow out of it.

- There is a root-and-fruit relationship between our heart and our behavior. That is, the heart controls everything we do and say.
- Lasting change always takes place through the pathway of the heart.
- Therefore, in personal growth and ministry, heart change is always our goal.

The Question of What Rules the Heart

Maybe you are thinking, *I understand what the Bible says about the heart controlling our behavior, but I don't know what I'm looking for as I examine the heart.* Our next passage will help us here. Turn to Ezekiel 14:1–5. Follow as I read.

Now, let me set the scene for you. The spiritual leaders of Israel have come to the prophet because they have questions that they want to ask God. But as they approach God, he recognizes that something is wrong with them. Look at the passage again. What is wrong with these men?

What is wrong with these men is idolatry. Notice what kind of idolatry. The passage says that they have idols in their hearts. This is deeper and more fundamental than cultural or religious idolatry. An idol of the heart is anything that rules us other than God.

Now, notice God's response. He says that because these men have idols in their hearts, he is going to answer them "in keeping with their great idolatry." God is saying, "Because you have idols in your hearts, the only thing I want to talk about is your idolatry." Why? Maybe they had important questions to ask God. Why would he refuse to talk about anything but the idols?

There is a phrase here that explains God's reaction to these men and explains much to us about how the heart functions. The passage says, "These men have set up idols in their hearts and put wicked stumbling blocks before their faces" (see v. 3).

Let me illustrate the principle for you. Put your hand up to your face so that you are looking through your fingers. What is happening to your vision? It is obstructed. The only way for your vision to be clear is for your hand to be removed. Here is the unbreakable connection:

idol in the heart ➔ stumbling block before the face

Now let me give you the core principle of this passage. It is the principle of inescapable influence. Whatever rules the heart will exercise inescapable influence over a person's life and behavior.

How does this relate to personal growth and ministry? Let's say you are trying to help a very controlling man who has damaged many relationships in his quest for power. You will not solve his problem by giving him good biblical instruction in communication and conflict resolution. Why? Because as long as the desire for control rules his heart, he will use whatever principles and skills he learns to establish even greater control over the people around him.

If we do not deal with what rules our hearts, we will use even the principles of the Word of God to serve our idols!

Let's examine how the principles of this passage apply to personal growth and ministry.

- Our hearts are always being ruled by someone or something.
- The most important question to ask when examining the heart is, "What is effectively and functionally ruling this person's heart in this situation?"
- Whatever controls my heart will control my reactions and responses to the people and situations in my life.
- The way God changes us is to recapture our hearts to serve him alone.
- The deepest issues of the human struggle are not issues of pain and suffering. The deepest issue is the issue of worship (What really rules my heart?) because what rules our hearts will control the way we respond to both suffering and blessing.

Let's consider two more passages that help us understand this issue. Turn to Romans 1:25.

Paul makes it very simple for us. He calls idolatry a great exchange. What Paul says here describes us all. We all tend to exchange worship and service of the Creator for worship and service of the creation. What a simple way to explain idolatry! This is what sin is about. The roots of sin in the heart are that we want and love the creation more than the Creator. What really rules our hearts in the situations and relationships of daily living is not love for God but a craving for some other thing. This exchange (Creator for creation) can take place in any situation or relationship in life. When it does, we will not do what God has called us to do.

The Matter of Treasure

The second passage we want to consider is Matthew 6:19–24.

Here Christ uses the word *treasure* to describe what rules our hearts. A treasure is something valuable to us. We all live to gain, maintain, and enjoy our treasures. There are three treasure principles in this passage. The first is assumed, and the others are delineated quite clearly.

1. Everyone lives for some kind of treasure.
2. Whatever you treasure will control your heart. ("Where your treasure is, there your heart will be also.")
3. Whatever controls your heart will control your behavior. ("No one can serve two masters.")

The Bible and the Heart

One final consideration is necessary. Maybe you are thinking, *I know that heart change is the goal, but it seems impossible to know the heart. I can only see a person's behavior; I can't look into the heart.* Does it seem as if we are discussing the impossible? Then turn in your Bibles to Hebrews 4:12–13.

This passage is about the Bible, and how God uses his Word in our lives. The writer of Hebrews says that the Bible is like God's great scalpel. It is able to cut through all the layers of who we are and what we're doing to expose our hearts. Hebrews says that the Bible reveals and judges our hearts' thoughts and motives. These are the two most fundamental things our hearts do: our hearts think and our hearts purpose. They interpret and they desire.

What you and I do is always shaped by these thoughts and motives. They control what we do with the relationships and situations we encounter in daily life.

Here's the encouragement of this passage: Although you cannot see a person's heart, Scripture will expose it to you. The Bible by its very nature is heart-revealing. For that reason, Scripture must be our central tool in personal growth and ministry. It alone can expose and analyze where change needs to take place in our hearts. Remember, heart change *must* take place if we really want changes in our behavior to last.

THE BIG QUESTION: What is your biggest problem?

CPR

Concepts

1. The heart is active. It controls our behavior.

2. Whatever rules the heart exercises inescapable influence over life and behavior. Your heart is always ruled by something.

3. God's Word alone is able to expose and judge the heart.

Personalized

1. If I am committed to personal change and growth, I must be committed to a biblical examination of my heart.

2. In the situations and relationships of my everyday life I must constantly ask, "What is really ruling my heart?"

3. I must always study the Word of God with an eye toward my heart, always asking what the passage reveals about my thoughts and motives. (What is really ruling me?)

Related to others

1. As I minister to others, I want to be an instrument of heart change.

2. Heart change is always the result of the careful ministry of God's Word to a particular person in a specific situation.

3. I must not attempt to manipulate or control the behavior of others. I must leave room for God to work lasting change in their hearts.

Make It Real

1. How will the truths of this lesson shape your prayers about ministry opportunities?

2. Give some examples (good and bad) of your heart overflowing in your words and deeds. What kind of fruit stapling have you tried? When have you seen real change?

3. What are some idols and treasures that challenge the Lord for control of your heart? How have they shaped your interpretations of certain events and relationships in your life?

4. How can God use the things he has taught you in this lesson to enable you to help someone else?

5. Write your best definition of what it means to function as one of God's instruments of change in the life of another.

LESSON 3

Understanding Your Heart Struggle

DISCUSS HOMEWORK

REVIEW

CONCEPTS AND OBJECTIVES

Concept: The cause of my struggle is not the people or the situations in my life, but the "heart" that I bring to those relationships and circumstances.

Personalized: I must live with a willingness to examine the true ruling desires of my heart and to learn how those desires shape my responses to people and circumstances.

Related to others: My effectiveness as one of God's instruments of change involves helping others to recognize and confess what really rules them.

LESSON CONTENT

This lesson focuses on two Scripture passages that are windows on the heart struggle of every human being. These passages show us how we end up worshipping and serving the creation rather than the Creator. They demonstrate that what rules the heart powerfully controls how we see and respond to what is around us.

Fights and Quarrels

Turn in your Bibles to James 4:1–10. This passage is a detailed illustration of the principles we considered in lesson 2. James starts with fruit and works down to roots in the heart.

The fruit that James wants us to examine is present in all of our lives. It is human conflict. All of us have a shocking amount of conflict in our lives. It may be fighting over who sits where in the car or who gets into the bathroom first or who eats the last chocolate chip cookie. It may be a discouraging disagreement between a husband and wife or a boss and a worker. James wants us to examine this fruit of conflict by asking, "What causes it?"

Notice that James calls us to do something very different from what we normally do when we are angry. We typically look outside ourselves to explain our anger. ("He makes me so angry!" "If you were the mother of these kids, you'd understand!" "This traffic drives me nuts!") James tells us that if we want to understand our anger, we must examine our hearts.

James says that the "fights and quarrels" we have so constantly are rooted in the desires of our hearts. He says, "Don't they come from the desires that battle within you?" In short, James says, "You fight because of what you want." What a radical perspective this is! People and situations do not make us angry. They only provide the occasion for our anger to express itself.

It is important to understand what James says about the desires of our hearts.

- He does not say it is wrong to desire. When you quit desiring, you are dead! The capacity to desire is God-given and not wrong in itself.
- James does not say that these fights and quarrels are only caused by evil desires.

According to James, how do the desires of our hearts explain the conflicts in our lives? The key phrase is found after the word *desires*. James says that our fights and quarrels come from desires that are waging war within our hearts. What is the sole purpose of war? It is control. You see, it is not the fact that we desire that is the problem, but the fact that certain desires wage war in our hearts until they effectively and functionally rule us.

Consider this for a moment. If my heart is ruled by a certain desire, there are only two ways I can respond to you. If you are helping me get what I want, I will be very happy with you and our relationship. But, if you stand in the way of what I want, I will experience anger, frustration, and discouragement when I am with you. My problem is not you or the situation we are in together. My problem is that a legitimate desire has taken over my heart and now is in control. It has so much power that it is no longer legitimate. So my response to you is not shaped by God and what he says is best but by a certain desire that now controls my heart.

Scripture uses the term *idolatry* to describe a desire that rules my heart. My own idolatry is what causes me to be angry. You stand in the way of what I crave, so I lash out against you in anger. This battle over who or what will rule the heart goes on in all of us all the time. What controls the heart will control the behavior. There is no situation or relationship where this battle is not taking place because we all tend to "exchange worship and service of the Creator for worship and service of the created thing."

How Desires Take Control

Maybe you're thinking, *How do the normal desires of daily living take control of the heart?* Let's consider the steps:

1. Desire: "I want." Nothing wrong here yet.
2. Demand: "I must." The desire is no longer an expression of love for God and man, but something I crave for myself.
3. Need: "I will." Something desirable is now seen as essential. I am convinced that I cannot live without it.
4. Expectation: "You should." This is where my relationships begin to be affected. If I really believe that this is a need, then it seems right to expect that you will meet my need if you really love me.
5. Disappointment: "You didn't!" Here the anger breaks out and becomes personal. You are standing in the way of what rules my heart.
6. Punishment: "Because you didn't, I will . . . ." I respond to you in anger (silent treatment, hurtful words, vengeance, or violence).

It is important to understand the core principle of this passage, which is found in verse 4. When James says, "You adulterous people," he is not changing the subject. He is explaining why we all struggle with anger. Here is the central principle of this passage: Human conflict is rooted in spiritual adultery. My problem is not sinful people or difficult situations. My problem is that I give the love that belongs to God to someone or something else. My problem is idolatry.

Now, notice the turning point of the passage. Change does not start with trying to control my anger or being careful with my communication or remembering conflict resolution principles. James says that change begins as we "submit to God." Only as we confess and forsake our idolatry (desires that have come to rule us) will we live in peace with one another. We are called to "come near to God," and we are promised that he will in turn come near to us.

James says that change involves two things:

1. "Wash your hands." This has to do with changes in our behavior.
2. "Purify your hearts." This has to do with ridding our hearts of idols.

It is almost impossible to overstate the importance of what this passage teaches. James is essentially saying that you cannot keep the Second Great Command ("Love your neighbor as yourself") if you have not submitted to the First Great Command ("Love the Lord your God . . .").

A Real Life Illustration

Powerful Emotions and Powerful Desires

Another passage explains how our hearts struggle and how that struggle shapes our response to people and situations. Turn to Galatians 5:13–26.

This passage falls into four sections: call, struggle, warning, and provision.

The call (v. 13) is that we would "serve one another in love." Yet we all recognize how hard this is to do. From the argument over the last cookie to the couple who are convinced they can no longer live together, we find it hard to lovingly serve one another. It is easier for us to demand. It is easier for us to wait to be served. It seems more natural to fight for our place and our rights.

Why is serving others such a struggle? Why does it seem so hard? Why does it demand such sacrifice? Why do so few of us really go through life with an attitude of service?

To understand our difficulty with the call, we have to understand the struggle that lies behind it.

The struggle takes place in our hearts. It is our struggle with our own sinful nature. We struggle because God has not yet completed his work in us. Our struggle is with indwelling sin. In times when we are called to serve another, we indulge our sinful nature instead.

To indulge something means to give in to it or feed it. When you indulge your appetite, you eat. So, instead of giving in to God's call, we give in to the desires and demands of the sinful nature.

Verse 24 explains what Paul means when he talks about indulging the sinful nature. It means that you give in to its passions and desires. This means that in certain relationships and situations my responses are not being controlled by the Lord and his will. Instead, I am being ruled by powerful emotions (passions) and powerful cravings (desires). So fear, anger, discouragement, the desire to belong, the desire to be affirmed, and so on, set the agenda for my behavior rather than the Lord.

This leads us to the warning in the passage. Paul warns us that we can destroy one another. We can smash another's hope. We can crush another's faith. We can break another's spirit. The fact is that our actions do make a difference. Our responses to one another are either productive or destructive. It is unbiblical to say that the unkind word, the thoughtless action, or the selfish initiative make no difference. We are always influencing one another, one way or the other.

God's Provisions for the Struggle

How will we ever defeat the sinful nature? How will we find the strength to fight its control? How can we say no to the powerful emotions and desires that rise up within us? The answer to these questions is not found in our strength but in God's provision.

Paul directs us to two things God gives so that we can say no to the passions and desires of the sinful nature and serve one another in love.

1. We have been crucified with Christ. (See v. 24.) Paul is calling us to remember our union with Christ. This union means that when Christ died, I died. When Christ rose, I, too, rose to a new life where sin's power over me has been forever broken. Now I have the power to resist its control.

   This means that we do not have to be ruled by powerful emotions and desires. We can resist them and respond to one another in servant love.
2. We have been given the Warrior Spirit. (See Galatians 5:16–18.) Why this name? Because the Holy Spirit, who dwells in us, fights on our behalf. Paul is literally saying here that the Spirit is an adversary who stands opposed to the sinful nature. God knew that our natures are so weak, and the conflict within so powerful, that he could not leave us to ourselves. He sent his Spirit to literally live inside us so that, by his power, we would be able to defeat the passions and desires of our sinful nature.

   Because the power of sin has been broken and the Holy Spirit has been given, we can say no to powerful emotions and powerful desires and be free to serve one another in love.

THE BIG QUESTION: As you deal with your daily situations and relationships, what things tend to control your heart?

CPR

Concepts

1. What a person does and says is not caused by the people and situations around him.

2. A person's behavior is always controlled by the desires that rule his heart.

3. We have been united with Christ and indwelt by the Holy Spirit so that we can say no to the passions and desires of the sinful nature.

Personalized

1. When attempting to understand my emotions, words, and actions, I must always examine my own heart.

2. I must learn to ask myself what emotions and desires control me in the various relationships and situations of daily life.

3. I must learn to affirm my identity in Christ and rely on the indwelling Holy Spirit as I seek to serve others in love.

Related to others

1. I must not blame people or circumstances for my emotions, words, and actions.

2. I must always remember that the desires that rule my heart will shape the way I relate to the people in my life. I must constantly ask myself if those relationships are characterized by demanding or serving.

3. I must be committed to helping people remember who they are in Christ as they struggle with temptations to indulge the sinful nature.

Make It Real

1. Study the following passages to see how Jesus looked beyond external behavior to the heart.

Passage	Situation	What Jesus discerned about the heart
Matt. 8:23–27	Disciples in boat with Jesus	
Matt. 12:38–39	Pharisees request a sign.	
Matt. 16:21–23	Peter rejects the idea that Jesus will suffer.	
Matt. 22:15–22	Pharisees try to trap Jesus.	
Mark 7:1–23	Pharisees and "unclean" hands	
Mark 10:17–23	Rich young man	
Luke 9:46–48	Dispute over who is greatest	
Luke 10:38–42	Mary and Martha	
Luke 15:1–2, 11–32	Parable of the Lost Son	
John 4:1–26	Woman at the well	
John 6:1–14, 25–58	Feeding of the five thousand	

Passage	Situation	What Jesus discerned about the heart
John 8:1–11	Woman caught in adultery	
John 13:1–17	Jesus washes disciples' feet	
John 21:15–19	Jesus reinstates Peter	

2. Examine your heart in the light of these passages. If Christ were talking to you, what would he seek to expose? Where is he calling you to fundamental heart change? Pray about these things.

LESSON 4

Following the Wonderful Counselor

DISCUSS HOMEWORK

REVIEW

CONCEPTS AND OBJECTIVES

Concept: Effective personal ministry seeks to be part of what the Lord is doing in the lives of others by modeling the way he has worked in us.

Personalized: I must examine the way I seek to stimulate change in those around me. Are the things I do consistent with the example of the Wonderful Counselor?

Related to others: I must think redemptively about my relationships. That is, I always look for the opportunities he is giving me to be part of his work of change.

LESSON CONTENT

Have you ever known that a friend needed to change, but you simply did not know how to help? Have you ever tried to help and felt like you made things worse? Have you ever felt like you wanted to help someone, but you were in over your head?

When our culture thinks about helping a person change, it usually thinks in formal and professional terms. If you accept that model, you will probably conclude two things:

1. That the Bible doesn't say much about how to help a person change.
2. That the average Christian has no business trying to help someone change.

Many Christians have bought into the cultural model and, as a result, become passive and uninvolved in the needs that surround them. It's not that they don't care. It's that they don't know what to do, and if they did, they don't think they should do it.

Called to Be Ambassadors

Scripture gives us a very different model. First, it calls each of us to function as Christ's ambassadors. An ambassador is a representative.

This is exactly what we are all called to be in all of our relationships. We are placed in these relationships not only so that our lives would be happy and satisfying, but more importantly so that we would represent the Lord as he is working change in others' lives.

The work of an ambassador includes three important points of focus. As an ambassador I will represent:

1. The message of the King. An ambassador is always asking, "What does my Lord want to communicate to this person in this situation?"
2. The methods of the King. This is the "how" of the ambassadorial calling. How does the Lord work change in our lives? What are his methods? I want to work as he has worked.
3. The character of the King. Here I am focusing on "why" the Lord does what he does. I want to faithfully represent his attitudes.

Happily, the second thing that Scripture does is to liberally display the work of the King for us. As we read the Bible, we hear his message over and over again (Matthew 5–7; Luke 15–18). As we read the Bible, we are confronted with his methods again and again (Luke 9:18–27; 10:25–37; John 3:1–21; 4:1–26). And the pages of Scripture are filled with the beauty of his character (Ephesians 4:29–5:2; Philippians 2:1–12; 1 Peter 2:23). These three things define how we can be useful instruments in the hands of Christ, our Model and our King. We accept our calling as ambassadors and faithfully seek to represent his message, methods, and character wherever and with whomever he places us.

See figure 4-1 on the next page. This illustration is meant to capture what it means to function as one of Christ's ambassadors of change in someone's life. Let me walk through the illustration with you.

First, you will notice that on the left side of the page are the words "Negative Fruit." This pictures the problems that get us involved in personal ministry. God opens our eyes to a harvest of bad fruit in a person's life. It may be a broken relationship. It may be anger, fear, or discouragement. It may be an act of gossip or vengeance. God allows us to see someone thinking, behaving, or responding in a wrong way. Or perhaps a struggling person reveals these things to us and asks for our help. However it happens, we are exposed to a harvest of bad fruit in someone's life.

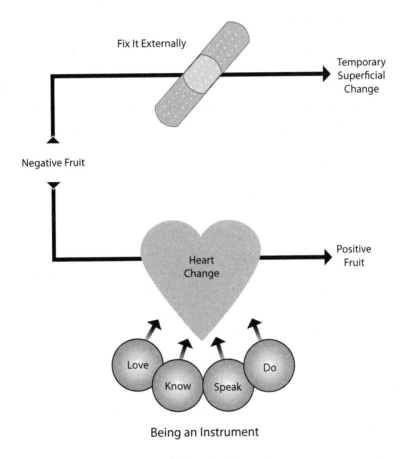

Figure 4-1.
Serving as an Instrument of Change

On the right side of the diagram are the words "Positive Fruit." This is our goal. Our purpose is to be used of God to produce a harvest of good fruit in the person's life, even though he or she may remain in the exact same situation with the exact same people.

The bandage at the top middle of the diagram summarizes the goal most people have when they seek help. Yes, they want things to change, but they seldom have their hearts in view. They basically have an externalistic view of change. They want a change in their circumstances, a change in another person, or a change in their emotions. They think that if "things" would change, they would be much better. But the result, as the illustration shows, is seldom more than temporary and superficial change. It's true that there are often elements in a situation that need to be changed, but we cannot stop there. Our goal is to lead people to a deeper, fuller view of change. This is why the heart (with the arrows pointing to it) is at the bottom middle of the diagram. We believe that lasting change always takes place through the pathway of the heart. The heart is our target. Heart change is our goal.

We finally come to the four circles with the heading "Being an Instrument." The four words in the circles—*Love, Know, Speak, Do*—describe God's way of change. This is our model for functioning as an instrument of real heart change in a person's life. This model takes seriously our need for heart change and our need to follow the example of Christ.

As you look at the diagram, don't think that you are learning a four-step process. The four circles represent four aspects of a personal ministry relationship, four ways to get involved in someone's life. As God gives you ministry opportunities, you will be doing all four things simultaneously.

Let's examine each element separately.

Love

The *Love* function points out the importance of relationship to the process of change. You could argue biblically that change always takes place in the context of a relationship. Theologians call this a covenantal model of change. God comes and makes a covenant with us. He commits himself to being our God, and he takes us as his people. And in the context of that relationship, he accomplishes his work of radically changing us.

As we understand the work of God in our own lives, we realize that our relationship to him is not a luxury. It is a necessity. It provides the only context in which the lifelong process of change can take place in us. In the same way, we are called to build strong and godly relationships with one another. God's purpose for these relationships is that they would be workrooms for him. It is important, therefore, that we learn how to build relationships in which his work of change can thrive.

Know

Know has to do with really getting acquainted with the people around us. Many of the people we think we know we really don't know. We know facts about them (who their spouse is, where they work, some likes and dislikes, their children, etc.), but we really don't know the person inside the skin. Our relationships are often trapped in the casual, and because of this, our opportunities to minister effectively are limited.

Knowing a person really means knowing the heart. When I say I am getting to know you better, I'm not gaining a more intimate understanding of your nose or arm! I mean that I know more about your beliefs and goals, your hopes and dreams, your values and desires. If I know you, I will be able to predict what you will think and how you will feel in a given situation. A friendship is really the connection of hearts.

Christ was so committed to an accurate knowledge of our hearts that he entered our world and lived here for thirty-three years. He faced everything we face so that we could come to him knowing that he understands our struggle.

So, the Know function gets us below the surface of the casual. It teaches us how to gather the information necessary to know a person at the level of his heart. And as we get to know the person, we help him to know himself more accurately and clearly.

Speak

Speak involves bringing God's truth to bear on this person in this situation. To do this we need to ask, "What does God want this person to see that he or she is not seeing? How can I help him see it?"

The Gospels are full of brilliant examples of the way Christ helped people to see the truth. Through stories and questions, he broke through their spiritual blindness and helped them to see the reality of who they were and the glory of what he could do for them.

Speaking the truth in love does not mean making grand pronouncements. Rather, it means helping a person to see his life clearly. For lasting change to take place, a person must see himself accurately in the mirror of God's Word. It is also vital that he accurately sees God, and the resources for change he has provided.

Do

Finally, we must help the person to *Do* something with what he has learned—to apply the insights God has given to his or her daily life and relationships. Insight alone is not change; it is the beginning of change. The insights God gives us about who we are, who he is, what he has provided for us, and what he has called us to do must be applied to practical, specific realities of everyday life.

Christ calls us not just to be hearers of his Word but to be active doers as well. As Christ's ambassadors, we are meant to help others respond in practical, personal ways to this call.

Something further needs to be said about the Love-Know-Speak-Do model of personal ministry. This is not only an aspect of the ministry of the local church but a lifestyle to which God has called each one of us. God has called us to be the life-changing instruments of his grace in each situation and in every relationship. This lifestyle will work in the formal counseling office as well as in an informal conversation with a struggling Christian friend. This ministry model can be easily adapted to whatever opportunities God gives you to function as one of his instruments of change.

THE BIG QUESTION: Right now, where has God positioned you to be one of his instruments of change?

CPR

Concepts

1. God calls us to be ambassadors, representing his message, methods, and character (2 Corinthians 5:14–21).

2. Ambassadors get from negative fruit to positive fruit not by fixing problems externally but by heart change.

3. The Love-Know-Speak-Do model follows Christ's example of how to do this (John 13:34).

Personalized

1. In all of my relationships, I must remember that I am Christ's ambassador.

2. I must examine my goals for my relationships. Am I solely motivated by my own personal happiness? Do I respond to others with a desire to encourage God's work of change in their lives?

3. I must examine my commitment to the message, methods, and character of the King.

Related to others

1. I must learn to look at all of my relationships redemptively, keeping an eye out for God-given moments of ministry.

2. It is important to use the Love-Know-Speak-Do model as a way to examine the quality of the relationships God has given me.

3. In my relationships, I must always remember that I am called to be God's instrument. God alone changes people.

Make It Real

1. What are some reasons why external change is appealing to us as human beings? Why does God seek heart change?

2. How has God dealt with you according to the Love-Know-Speak-Do model? How have others done Love-Know-Speak-Do with you? Pick a specific instance.

3. Reflect (using this model) on two or three relationships in your life. Where are they weak? Where are they strong? Have you been functioning as an ambassador? Pray that God would use these truths to shape the way you serve in these relationships.

4. Personal Ministry Opportunity

Throughout the rest of *Instruments in the Redeemer's Hands*, you will begin a process in which you will apply what you have learned about Love, Know, Speak, and Do. The Make It Real section of every lesson will help you to think about a specific personal setting where you can apply what you learn. We hope that you will find this challenging and exciting. Thinking about a particular ministry opportunity can spur you to make changes in your relationships in some everyday situation.

First, choose a setting where you want to concentrate your attention. You could choose a formal or an informal relationship, a 1:1 relationship, or a small group.

- You could choose a setting whose stated purpose is Christian nurture: a Sunday school class, a Bible study group, a discipling relationship, or a small group.
- You could choose a person you live with: a family member or roommate.

- You could choose a more casual setting: a friendship, a conversation after church or over coffee, conversations at work over lunch, contacts in your neighborhood or at an athletic event.
- You could choose a work group: a board of elders or deacons, the choir, a missions or worship committee, a team of Sunday school teachers, an evangelistic team, coworkers on a task force, or a study group at school.

Whatever you choose, seek to become more biblically intentional in your communication.

Second, describe and analyze the setting and the person or people involved. Who are the members (including you!)? What actually happens when you get together? What are the typical communication patterns? If you are focusing on a small group, what is its history? What are its stated or assumed purposes? What is the leadership structure, formal or informal? What roles do people fill? What agenda or goals—stated or unstated—operate in each person and in the group as a whole? What are the current strengths and weaknesses of the group from a biblical standpoint?

Third, as you work through the rest of the lessons, begin to strategize. Design a plan for ministry on the basis of what you have been studying and thinking. How will you bring about an increasingly biblical ministry? How will you act and speak differently? What does the Bible say about you and the relationship or group? Allow the teaching you will receive in lessons 5–12 to inform you as you take advantage of this ministry opportunity.

Fourth, pray! As you study each lesson, don't simply think of the truths as strategies for happier relationships. See them as a means to see your own need for change and your dependence upon Christ to live in a way that evidences him. You may want to ask two or three people to pray for you in this process. (This exercise was developed by David Powlison as a class assignment in "Counseling in Everyday Life." It has been adapted for this curriculum).

LESSON 5

Love I: Building Relationships in Which God's Work Will Thrive

DISCUSS HOMEWORK

1. What does the Bible say about how people change?

2. What four elements of the biblical model of personal ministry were presented in lesson 4? What did you learn about your strengths and weaknesses?

REVIEW

In lesson 1 we learned that we all need *help:*

1. Human beings need truth outside themselves to understand life.
2. Influence and advice always carry a moral agenda.
3. Spiritual blindness affects us all. We need to be willing to give help and receive it.

In lesson 2 we learned that the *heart* is the target:

1. The idols that rule the heart will shape the life and behavior.
2. The Bible is God's mirror to reveal our hearts, so we must be committed to examining our hearts biblically.
3. You must change the root (the heart) to change the fruit (behavior).

In lesson 3 we learned about the *hope* in our union with Christ:

1. People and situations do not control what we say and do.
2. Our heart's desires control our behavior.
3. When we are united with Christ and indwelt by the Holy Spirit, we can say no to the passions and desires of the sinful nature.

In lesson 4 we learned that we are *ambassadors:*

1. Our ministry will be effective when it reflects the way the Wonderful Counselor works in our lives.
2. As God's ambassadors, we are to represent his message, methods, and character.
3. The Love-Know-Speak-Do model reflects Christ's example and helps us gauge our effectiveness in relationships.

CONCEPTS AND OBJECTIVES

Concept: God always changes people in the context of relationships based on love.

Personalized: I must build relationships in which love provides a context for God's work of change.

Related to others: Biblical love demands a higher agenda for my relationships than making myself and the other person happy.

LESSON CONTENT

What would you say in response to this question: "What role do relationships play in ministry?" Are the relationships God gives us mere luxuries, wonderful gifts from a loving God to bring us happiness? Or does the Bible present a higher agenda? God's plan for our relationships is what this lesson is about.

God's relationship with us is loving and redemptive. Our salvation in Christ opens the door for us to have relationships with others that reflect those qualities. Perhaps you are thinking, *I understand the words, but I am not sure what you mean.* To say that God wants our relationships to be loving and redemptive means three things:

1. That he has a higher goal for our friendships than our present, personal happiness
2. That he wants our relationships to provide a context for his ongoing work of change in and through us.
3. That we need to build relationships that promote and encourage this work of change.

Our Relationship with God

There is no better way to understand the important role of relationships than to consider the way Christ works in our own lives. Look at figure 5-1, which captures the importance of relationship in God's work of personal change.

The pathway represents our lives. The two doors, labeled justification and adoption, represent the two things Christ did to bring us into relationship with God and make us his children. These words explain how we enter into relationship with God.

In justification by faith, God declares us to be righteous based on the perfect life, death, and resurrection of Christ. In justification, Christ's righteousness is credited to our accounts. Justification is important because our sin separates us from God. Justification removes our sin and gives us Christ's righteousness, making us acceptable to God and thus able to have a relationship with him.

Adoption also involves our relationship with God. Not only does God justify us; he adopts us. He welcomes us into his family with all the rights and privileges of being his child. Justification and adoption give us a full and complete relationship with God.

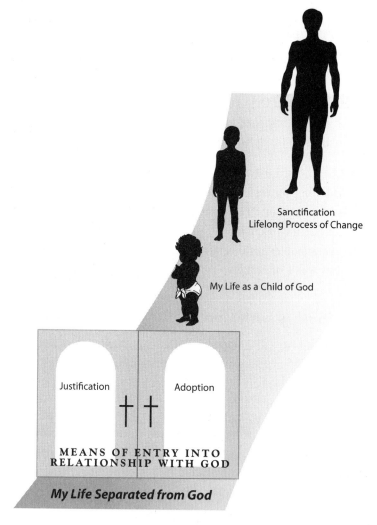

Sanctification
Lifelong Process of Change

My Life as a Child of God

Justification

Adoption

MEANS OF ENTRY INTO
RELATIONSHIP WITH GOD

My Life Separated from God

Figure 5-1.
The Relational Foundation for Ministry:
Salvation as Our Model

As a result of justification and adoption, are we okay? This is a trick question. If we are talking about our standing or relationship with God, the answer is yes. Nothing needs to be added to Jesus' work. If we are talking about our condition as people, the answer is no. We still struggle with sin, and there is still radical change that needs to take place in us, so that we can be what God has chosen us to be and do what he has chosen us to do (pictured by the baby maturing into an adult). That lifelong process of change is called sanctification. Sanctification is the process by which God actually makes us what he legally declared us to be in justification—holy.

God doesn't justify and adopt us because we are okay but precisely because we are not okay. He knows that lasting change will take place in us only when we are in a personal relationship with him. In his love, he makes that relationship a reality. Only those who have a relationship with God through justification and adoption will undergo the radical change process of progressive sanctification.

The way Christ loves us and works to change us is our model as we love others and work with them. We, too, want to begin by building relationships of love, grace, and trust with others. This is a covenantal view of change. In the biblical model, relationships are not a luxury but a necessity. They are where redemptive activity always takes place.

Let's recap:

- Redemptive activity always takes place in the context of relationships.
- God's first step in changing us is to draw us into relationship with him.
- Our relationships are an essential part of the work of change God is completing in us and in others.

Four Elements of a Loving Relationship

Look at figure 5-2. The oval represents one of your relationships. The four words summarize four ways to demonstrate love to someone and build a relationship that promotes God's work of change.

1. Enter the person's world.
2. Incarnate the love of Christ.
3. Identify with suffering.
4. Accept with agenda.

We will discuss each of these elements of love in detail.

1. Enter the Person's World

How do we build a personal ministry relationship? How can we be used by God to help people to seek his help? Why do we tend to miss so many ministry opportunities?

When we seek to capture God-given opportunities for ministry, we have to recognize the entry gates God gives us. A gate is a means of entry from one thing to another. What are the entry gates from a casual relationship to a life-changing ministry relationship?

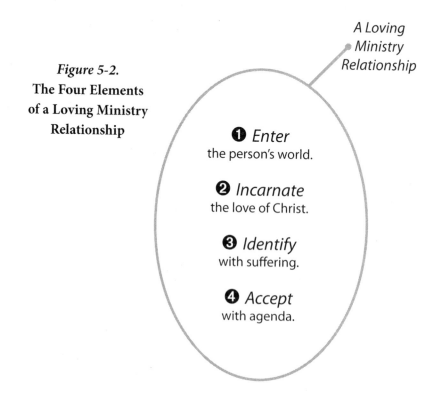

Figure 5-2.
The Four Elements of a Loving Ministry Relationship

A Loving Ministry Relationship

❶ *Enter* the person's world.

❷ *Incarnate* the love of Christ.

❸ *Identify* with suffering.

❹ *Accept* with agenda.

Let's talk about what an entry gate is not.

- It is not the problem that the person wants to talk about.
- It is not a situation or circumstance in his life.
- It is not another person or a problem in a relationship.

No, an entry gate is this particular person's experience of the situation, problem, or relationship. To recognize the entry gate, we need to ask, "What is this person struggling with in the midst of the situation?" Or, "What has this person in its grip right now?"

Here is an example. A woman has been married for fifteen years and has three children. She awakens one morning to find that her husband is gone. In a note, he announces that he has left the marriage. He has fallen in love with someone else, taken his clothes, emptied the bank account, and hired a lawyer. She calls you on the phone. Ask yourself, what has this woman in its grip? What is she struggling with right now? The obvious answer is fear. She is flooded with terrifying questions, the scariest being, "Why would God let this happen to me?"

In this situation, fear is the entry gate. It is a wonderful opportunity to show love and build a ministry relationship with this woman. So often we address a problem and miss the person in the middle of his or her unique struggle. We address situations and miss the war for the heart going on inside. However, when we recognize these entry gate opportunities and speak to them, people respond, "This person has heard me. This person understands me. I want more of this kind of help." This is the power of a loving relationship.

Remember, an entry gate is not the problem or situation itself but the way in which this person is struggling with the problem. (It might be fear, anger, guilt, anxiety, hopelessness, aloneness, envy, discouragement, desires for vengeance, etc.)

Three things will result from recognizing and responding to the entry gate issues:

1. The building of horizontal trust—the person feels understood and is therefore ready to trust you and tell you more.

2. The strengthening of vertical hope—as I represent God's sympathetic, understanding love and show how the Bible speaks to the deepest issues of an experience, the person will grow in her hope in the Lord's presence, promises, and power.
3. The beginning of a commitment to the process of change—the person says, "This has already been helpful. I want more of this kind of help."

How do you get beyond the problem and connect with the person? How do you recognize an entry gate issue? Here are three ways to identify the person's particular struggle in the midst of the situation.

1. Listen for emotive words. ("I am so scared." "I am totally discouraged." "This makes me so angry!")
2. Listen for interpretive words. ("I guess I deserve this." "This always happens to me." "God just doesn't hear me.")
3. Listen for self talk. ("I am such a failure." "I'm tired of being such a doormat!" "I feel like quitting altogether.")

Here are some entry gate questions you might ask this woman as you talk with her and build a relationship. (It would be unlikely that you would ask all these questions at once, especially when she first calls you.)

"What came into your mind when you read the note?"
"What are you struggling with most right now?"
"Are you facing something you thought you would never face? What are you feeling?"
"What are you afraid of right now?"
"Are you feeling angry? Where is that a real struggle?"
"How are you connecting with God right now? Do you have any sense of who he is and what he is doing?"
"Do you feel hopeless? Do you feel like God is asking you to do the impossible as you deal with this?"
"What questions do you wish you could ask your husband?"
"What questions do you wish you could ask God?"
"When you can't sleep, what thoughts keep you awake?"
"What part of this situation is getting to you the most?"
"Do you find yourself struggling with regrets?"

There is no shortage of ministry opportunities around us. Our real problem is that we do not know how to take advantage of them all. But we can learn to recognize these opportunities and use them to build loving relationships that encourage God's work of change.

2. Incarnate the Love of Christ

How does God use us to change people? Is it only through the things we say? Is change simply a matter of confronting people with the truth and calling them to obey? Or does God use us in other ways?

Take a moment now to reflect on the people God has used in your life. In the space provided, write the ways God used them to change your life. No doubt God used their words—their conversation, advice, and confrontation. But what other aspects of the relationship did God use to encourage change in you? Highlight those nonverbal elements as you write.

If we are taking our role as ambassadors seriously, we have to say that God changes people not only through what we say but through who we are and what we do. During his ministry on earth Jesus said, "If you have trouble believing what I say, then look at the things I have done. They are all the evidence that you need" (paraphrase of passages; see John 14:11). As ambassadors, we are not only called to speak the truth but to incarnate it—to be real, living, flesh-and-blood illustrations of it. We are not just God's spokespersons; we are his evidence. Our transformed lives testify to the power of his grace to transform hearts. God will transform people not only through what we say but also through the way we display the love God has shown to us and to them. We want to incarnate his love in the relationships he has given us.

Turn to Colossians 3:15–17. Here is one of the New Testament's clearest calls to personal ministry. We are called to have Scripture so deeply a part of us that we are wise and thankful, and therefore constantly prepared to teach and admonish (confront) one another. But we really don't understand this passage if we start with verse 15. We must start with verse 12.

In these verses Paul uses a very important metaphor, the metaphor of clothing. Clothing is important because it covers us. Clothing identifies us. Clothing describes our function. Paul is reminding us that what we wear to moments of personal ministry is as important as what we say. ("Wear" here does not refer to physical clothes but the clothing of a Christlike character.) Essentially, Paul is saying, "If you are going to be involved in what I am doing in the lives of others, come dressed for the job."

What is that clothing? These are not just isolated items of character. The qualities listed here add up to the character of Christ. Paul is saying, "You are called to put on Christ as you minister to others." God changes people not simply because we have said the hard words of truth to them but because those strong words were said with compassion, kindness, humility, gentleness, patience, and love. When we do this, we actually become the physical evidence of the very things we are presenting to others. When this happens, we are not only incarnating truth; we are incarnating Christ, who is with us and our only hope.

The incarnational aspect of ministry is important because God uses who we are to convey his truth, as well as what we say. But our relationship with another person is important for another reason as well. In personal ministry, the sin of the person we are ministering to will be revealed in our relationship. If you are ministering to an angry person, at some point that anger will be directed at *you*. If you are in a relationship with a person who is struggling with trust, at some point she will distrust *you*. A depressed person will tell you he tried everything you are suggesting and it didn't work. You might think of it this way: you can't stand next to a puddle without eventually being splashed by the mud!

Galatians 6:1 says, "Brothers, if someone is caught in a sin, you who are spiritual should restore him gently. But watch yourself, or you also may be tempted." (See also 1 Timothy 4:16.) We need to watch our reactions to the people we are serving, since they will often sin against us in the same way they sin against others. How do we respond when we are sinned against? Are we responding in love? As the person's sin and struggle become part of our experience, are we demonstrating the power of Christ's transforming grace in our response? Are we incarnating Christ as we deal with sin in our ministry and relationships?

Sometimes we will live up to our calling as Christ's ambassadors; at other times we will fail. Even then, we can minister effectively if we apply the gospel to our own lives by confessing our sin, asking forgiveness from God (and the other person, if appropriate) and claiming God's strength to serve him faithfully.

Remember, we are called to be ambassadors. An ambassador not only faithfully delivers the message of the King but incarnates his character as well. Personal ministry to suffering sinners will always mean sacrifice and suffering for us, so we must be aware of our responses to those trials. In the midst of ministry struggle, are we representing the King well? Are we willing to die to ourselves to see life in this other person? We are not only called to be a conduit of God's truth but an evidence of it as well.

THE BIG QUESTION: Are you building relationships in which God's work of change can thrive?

CPR

Concepts

1. Change takes place in the context of relationships.

2. People's struggles provide entry gates that help us build relationships promoting God's work of change.

3. God uses not only what we say, but how we incarnate the love of Christ to encourage change in others' lives.

Personalized

1. Are my relationships motivated by a desire for personal happiness or a desire for God's work of change?

2. Do I search for (and take advantage of) the entry gate opportunities God gives me?

3. Do I seek not only to be a spokesman for the transforming power of God's grace but the evidence of it as well?

Related to others

1. Right now, where is God revealing the struggles of others to me? Am I entering these gates of opportunity?

2. What motivates me most in my current relationships—God's work of change or my own idea of self-centered happiness?

3. In my current relationships, where is God giving me opportunities to demonstrate (by my character and my living) God's power to transform hearts?

Make It Real

1. As you think about your Personal Ministry Opportunity, how might you revise your goals? In what ways have your goals been less than redemptive? In what ways have you either failed to accept the person or given up on a godly agenda for change? Make your responses a matter of consistent prayer.

2. What entry gates into the experience of the person or group have you chosen? Write down some questions that would help you enter the person's or group's world with understanding and love.

3. What might it look like for you to incarnate Christ's love to that person? Try to think of ways that don't involve words! What character qualities do you need to exhibit? Think about examples where others have done this for you.

LESSON 6

Love II: Building Relationships in Which God's Work Will Thrive

DISCUSS HOMEWORK

REVIEW

1. What entry gate opportunities did God give you this week? How did you handle them?

2. Where did God call you to incarnate his love? What was the situation? What did you do?

CONCEPTS AND OBJECTIVES

Concept: God calls us to suffer so that we would be qualified agents of his comfort and compassion.

Personalized: I need to ask, "Where has God led me through suffering and what has he taught me through it?"

Related to others: I need to look for the sufferers that God has placed in my path. Have I functioned in their lives as God's agent of comfort?

LESSON CONTENT

In this lesson we begin to look at the remaining two aspects of love in a ministry relationship pictured in figure 5-2:

3. Identify with Suffering

Have you ever gone through a hard time and felt completely alone? Have you ever, in the middle of suffering, wondered if you were the only one who had gone through such a thing? Have you ever thought, in the middle of difficulty, that the people around you didn't really care? Have you gone through things that made you wonder if God cared?

One of the predictable realities of life in a fallen world is suffering. It is everywhere around us. It has touched each of our lives. Suffering is both a tool of redemption and an occasion for great temptation. Suffering is the common ground of personal ministry. It is the thing we share with everyone we meet.

Turn to Hebrews 2:10–11. This passage points to the importance of recognizing the commonality of suffering. Notice once again that Christ is our model here. This passage is about how Christ, "the author of our salvation," identifies with us. It says that Christ is not ashamed to call us "brothers." Pay attention to the nature of this term. The title "brother" not only connotes family relationship; it connotes sibling relationship. A sibling is an equal. To say you are my brother means:

- We are in the same family.
- We are in a similar position in the family.
- We share the same life experiences because of that position.

This should be the character of our personal ministry. It does not have that "I stand above you as one who has arrived" character. The character of personal ministry is humility. It flows out of the humble recognition that we share an identity. We are not finished products. God has not completed his work in us. We stand as brothers in the middle of God's lifelong process of change. We are not this person's guru. We are not what he or she needs. Change will not happen simply because he is exposed to our wisdom and experiences. We share identity, we share experience, and we are of the same family.

But we need to go further here. Look back at the Hebrews passage. What is the center, the core of our brotherhood? What is the thing we have in common with Christ? The answer is suffering.

Notice that verse 10 says something very interesting (and a bit confusing) about Christ. It says that, like us, he was made perfect through suffering. The writer is explaining how Christ shares identity with us, and making a connection between Christ's life and ours. The connection is found in the words "should make the author of their salvation perfect through suffering." If we understand this connection, we will have a better understanding of our relationship to Christ and how he has called us to minister to others.

So think for a moment: how did suffering make Christ perfect? When he came to earth, wasn't he already perfect?

You see the connection illustrated in figure 6-1. The left side pictures the life of Christ on earth. Christ had lived in eternity as the perfect Son of God, yet something else was needed before he could go to the cross as the perfect Lamb for sacrifice. His perfection needed to successfully endure the test of life in this fallen world. Christ needed to face sin and suffering without sinning. So at the end of his earthly life, how was Christ "made perfect"? He was now not only the perfect Son of God, but he had a perfection that had successfully endured the test of suffering. He now had demonstrated his righteousness on earth, and he had done so through suffering.

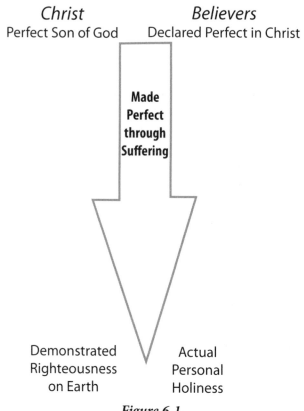

Figure 6-1.
Fellow Sufferers with Christ

Notice, as you look at the picture, the direct analogy to his work in us. We are declared perfect in Christ (justification), but through the process of suffering, we actually do become holy (sanctification). We are being made perfect through the same process that Christ went through. The identity we share is:

- Brothers
- Brothers in suffering
- Brothers in suffering that leads to holiness

This is also the identity we share with those we seek to love and help. Even with unbelievers, this shared brotherhood is our goal. We stand alongside one another. We are equals (brothers). We share the same experience (suffering). Our experience has the same goal (holiness). Let's consider how this identity should shape personal ministry:

It determines our posture in personal ministry. We do not stand above the people God calls us to serve. We stand alongside them as brothers, pointing them to the Father who is our source of help.

It determines the character of our ministry. Christ's humility in identifying with us in Hebrews 2 calls us to minister to others with a humble compassion (love). We are humble because we recognize that we, too, are people in the midst of God's process of change. And we are compassionate because we understand the realities of suffering that God uses to form us into his image.

It deals with the dependency issue. Often in personal ministry the people receiving help develop an unhealthy dependence on the people God is using in their lives. Here it is clear that we—the helpers—are not what the people need. In fact, we are just like them—people in need of God's ongoing work of change.

It redeems our experiences. All of the experiences God has brought us through, all of the things he has done for us, and all the ways he has changed us give us stories to tell. These personal stories allow us to present God's truth with a flesh-and-blood realism. This clarifies the truths being presented and gives hope to the hearer. My life becomes a window through which the person can see the grace and glory of the Lord.

4. Accept with Agenda

Here again we follow the example of Christ's love for us. The amazing grace that causes Christ to accept us into his family is not a grace that says we are okay. In fact, it is clear that the reason God extends his gracious acceptance to us is that we are everything but okay. As you and I enter God's family, we are people in need of radical personal change. So God's acceptance is not a call to relax but a call to work. We need to rest in his gift of grace, knowing that we do not have to earn acceptance with him. At the same time we need to realize that he calls us to participate in his lifelong work of change.

It is wrong to approach a struggling brother or sister with a critical, condemning, or self-righteous spirit. We must grant them the same grace and love that we received from God. At the same time, we do not want that offer of grace to be misunderstood. God's grace is always grace leading to change. Change is God's agenda in order that we would become partakers of his divine nature (2 Peter 1:4). As we seek to love people with the love of Christ, we must also hold before them God's call to change (Titus 2:11–3:8).

THE BIG QUESTION: Are you building relationships in which acceptance and a call to change are woven together?

CPR
Concepts

1. God ordains for us to suffer so that we would be qualified agents of his comfort and compassion.

2. God calls us to offer to others the same loving acceptance that he has given us. That acceptance always has change as its goal.

Personalized

1. Have I tended to hoard the comfort that God has given me?

2. Am I taking advantage of the opportunities God is giving me to comfort others with the comfort I have received from him?

3. Have I accepted God's call to participate in his process of life-long change?

Related to others

1. I need to look for the sufferers God has placed in my path.

2. What stories in my own life could be used as examples of the hope and comfort God gives us in suffering?

3. Right now, where is God giving me the opportunity to offer grace leading to change to another person?

How to Tell Your Story
A Biblical Model
2 Corinthians 1:3–11

1. *The Paradigm*: Viewing suffering redemptively

   - God, the source of true compassion (v. 3)
   - God's comfort has ministry in view (v. 4).
   - God's purposes for us to share in Christ's suffering (v. 5)
   - Even our suffering does not belong to us but to the Lord (v. 6).
   - The redemptive purpose in all of this is firm hope amid the harsh realities of a fallen world (v. 7).

2. *The Methodology*: Telling the stories of my struggle and the Lord's help

   - Tell your story in a way that breaks down the misconception that you are essentially different from the person you are helping (v. 8).
   - Always tell a completed story. It needs to include a difficult situation, your struggle in the midst of it, and how God helped you (v. 8).
   - As you tell your story, be honest in describing your struggles and failures (v. 9).
   - Be discerning and purposeful as you tell the story. Limit the amount of "gory" detail. The situation is not the focus but the God who met you in the middle of it (v. 9).

- Always tell your story in a way that makes God the key actor in the drama (v. 10).
- Tell your story with humility, admitting your continuing need for grace. Perhaps you will seek help (prayer) from the person to whom you are ministering (vv. 10–11).
- Always state that the story makes it clear that you are not what this person needs—God is. At best, you are one of God's instruments, who shares a daily need for his mercy and grace (v. 9).
- The goal of your story should always be worship. All true hope and comfort are rooted in a recognition of and thankfulness for God, his character, and his help. True hope does not come because you try to say something that will somehow make the person feel better (v. 11).

3. *Corollary Passage:* 2 Corinthians 4:7–18.

Make It Real

In 2 Corinthians 1:3–7, Paul makes it clear that our suffering and our experience of God's comfort have ministry in view. As we consider our own stories, we prepare ourselves to offer to others the same comfort we received from the Lord. We look back on our experiences not only to be thankful for what God has done but to encourage others to rely on the grace of Christ as they suffer. So let's celebrate God's comfort as we look back, but don't just celebrate! Let's look for the ways God has equipped us to bring his comfort to others. Ask him, "Is there someone I know who needs this comfort right now?"

1. List three situations in which God ministered his comfort to you in the midst of difficulty, suffering, or trial.

2. List the things you learned from these situations about God's presence, power, grace, love, promises, provisions, and so on.

3. In light of your Personal Ministry Opportunity, write out one of your "stories" using the guide from 2 Corinthians 1:3–11. Connect your story specifically to the person or group you have chosen as your focus. Pray for an opportunity to share it.

LESSON 7

Know I: Getting to Know People; Discovering Where Change Is Needed

DISCUSS HOMEWORK

REVIEW

1. Our hearts direct our lives, so God, in his redemptive love, is jealous for control of our hearts (lessons 1–3).
2. God calls us to be his ambassadors, representing his message, methods, and character to those around us (lesson 4).
3. Living as an ambassador means incarnating the Love of Christ, seeking to Know where change is needed in a person's life, being faithful to Speak the truth in love, and assisting people to Do what God has called them to do (lessons 4–6).

In this lesson, we move to the second of the four elements of a biblical model of personal ministry (Know). Here again, Christ is our model. Like him, we need to enter the world of the people we serve so that we can minister with the same sympathetic understanding we have received from him.

In this lesson, we will discuss ways in which our effectiveness as ambassadors is blunted when we don't know one another very well. We will learn to ask good questions that provide the information we need to minister to others in the places where change is really needed.

CONCEPTS AND OBJECTIVES

Concept: Wise people are not only people with the right answers but people who ask the right questions. We cannot get to the right answers without asking the right questions.

Personalized: I need to ask good questions and avoid making assumptions about people that keep me from doing so.

Related to others: I will look for opportunities to ask questions that move me beyond casual relationships and provide insight as to where ministry is needed.

LESSON CONTENT

Have you ever thought you knew someone well only to discover significant parts of his story that you did not know at all? Have you ever started to share a story from your own life and been interrupted by someone who said, "I know exactly what you mean!"—but clearly didn't? Right now, think of someone you believe you know very well. Try to identify some things about him or her that you don't know. Try to pinpoint the gaps in your understanding of his or her story.

This is what we will address in this lesson. We tend to live in terminally casual relationships. Yes, there are things that we know about one another (like who is married to whom, how many kids they have, who lives and works where, etc.). But the facts we know about people make us think that we know the human beings attached to those details. And because we assume that we know the people around us, we don't ask them good questions. This keeps our relationships trapped in the casual and sets the stage for all kinds of potential misunderstandings between others and ourselves. Today we'll consider the importance of knowing people and gathering the data necessary to minister effectively to those around us.

Christ the Data Gatherer

Perhaps you've looked at the title of this section and thought, *Aren't you stretching things a bit?* Yet even in this area, Christ is our chief example. Turn in your Bibles to Hebrews 4:14–16. Let's examine the logic of this passage together.

In verse 16, the writer of Hebrews says that in the midst of our struggles we can come to Jesus with confidence, knowing that we will receive mercy and grace appropriate to our need. It is right, then, to ask, "Why can we be so confident as we come to Christ for help?" Verse 15 tells us. Christ is able to sympathize with our weaknesses. The author uses powerful words here. The word for sympathy used here literally means to be touched by what has touched someone else or to be moved by what has moved someone else. This is more than pity, where we feel sorry for a person in a tough situation. This is understanding what it is like to be in that circumstance, coupled with a desire to help the person out.

The word for weaknesses is also very strong. It is almost untranslatable, but it is best understood as meaning "the human condition." The writer is saying that Jesus really does understand what it means to live in this fallen world. He understands all the things that push and pull us. He understands all the temptations we face. He understands how difficult and complicated our relationships are. He understands the limits of human strength and wisdom. He understands the difficult situations in which we find ourselves (disloyalty, betrayal, rejection, physical pain, aloneness, etc.). He understands the nature of families. Jesus has a complete understanding of our daily lives. He knows us!

How does Christ have such an accurate understanding of our existence? The passage clearly tells us with these words: "we have one who has been tempted in every way, just as we are—yet was without sin" (v. 15). Jesus understands us because he entered our world. For thirty-three years Jesus lived on earth, gathering data about the nature of our experience in a fallen world. He was literally "tempted in every way, just as we are." Christ's experiences during those years between his birth and the cross made him a high priest who could sympathize with our weaknesses. Because he entered our world, his understanding is firsthand and complete.

Like Christ, we want to understand people so that we can serve them. Unlike Christ, we do not usually move in with people physically. However, by taking time to ask good questions and listen well, we can begin to understand how they are responding to the situations and relationships they face daily. Our hope is that this would give others confidence to seek us out, to share more of their true struggles, and find, through us, the help that the Lord can give.

The Problem of Assumptions

Because we speak the same language, share many of the same experiences, live in the same community, and often attend the same church, it is easy to assume that we know more about people than we actually do. When we simply assume a similarity of thought, desire, and experience, we don't ask the questions we need to ask. This leads us to make invalidated assumptions about people and may lead us to minister to people who exist only in our minds!

For personal ministry to be effective, it must be based on a rich base of information gathered by asking good questions. Assuming that we know what we need to know and failing to ask appropriate questions almost always leads to misunderstandings that blunt and divert personal ministry. The principle here is, "Don't assume; ask." Then we can be sure that what we have concluded is actually true.

To make sure that our conclusions are valid, there are three things we must regularly do:

1. Ask people to define their terms. Human language is messy. We all define even familiar words in very different ways.
2. Ask people to clarify what they mean with concrete, real-life examples of the terms they have used.
3. Ask people to explain why they responded the way they did in the examples they have given you.

When we ask a person to define, clarify, and explain, we avoid the misunderstandings and false assumptions that can rob personal ministry of its effectiveness. Definition, clarification, and explanation are things we should ask for again and again.

Asking Good Questions

The primary way we get to know people is through the question-and-answer process. That makes it important to learn to ask good questions. Here are four principles to keep in mind.

1. *Always ask open-ended questions—questions that cannot be answered with a yes or no.* Yes-and-no questions do not give us much information because we do not know the thoughts behind the answer. For example, if I ask if you have a good marriage and you answer, "Yes," what have I learned? I haven't learned much because I do not know your definition of a good marriage.

Notice that open-ended questions cannot be answered without the person disclosing how he is thinking, what he wants, and what he is doing.

> 2. *Use a combination of survey and focused questions.* Survey questions scan the various areas of a person's life, looking at the person as a whole. Survey questions reveal themes and patterns. For example, a woman's relational problem with her husband may also exist with her parents and her children. It is not, therefore, an isolated problem but a theme in her life.
>
> Focused questions look intensively at one area of a person's life. Where survey questions scan widely, focused questions dig deeply into one area. Focused questions reveal roots and causes.

To get to know someone, we need to employ both kinds of questions. There are times when we need a wide-angle view, asking ourselves, "Does what I am seeing here exist elsewhere in this person's life?" We also need focused questions, asking ourselves, "What can I learn about what this person thinks, desires, and does by digging deeply into this one area of life?"

> 3. *Always remember that certain kinds of questions reveal certain kinds of information.* Ask yourself, "What do I need to know about this person to help him? What kind of question will uncover that information?"

There are essentially five classes of questions:

- What? questions are your most basic question. They uncover general information. ("What did you do?" "I talked to my wife.")
- How? questions reveal the way something was done. ("How did you talk to her?" "I yelled at her for fifteen minutes!")
- Why? questions uncover a person's purposes, desires, goals, or motivations. ("Why did you yell for so long?" "I wanted her to know how angry I was at what she had done.")
- How often? Where? questions. These questions reveal themes and patterns in a person's life. ("Where did this happen?" "At

the supper table. Suppers are hard. We are both tired. We have young children. Meals are not relaxing. The evening meal always seems to be tense for us.")

- When? questions. When questions uncover the order of events. ("Tell me exactly when you began to yell during supper." "In the middle of the chaos my wife said, 'Well, how was your day?' She was obviously annoyed because I hadn't asked about hers. I said, 'Do you care or are you just being nasty?' She said, 'Well, you're the only one here with an interesting and important life, right?' At that point I blew up.")

Each class of question uncovers different information and thereby broadens or deepens your understanding of what took place (the situation), how the person interacted with it (the thoughts and motives of the heart), and what he did in response (behavior). You will use these questions whether you are focusing on one area or surveying a person's life.

4. *Ask a progressive line of questions, in which each question is based on information uncovered in previous questions.* The flow of questions should be orderly and logical. Each question should broaden or deepen your understanding of whatever is being considered. You accomplish this by always asking yourself, "What do I not know about what I have just heard?" This question challenges you not to make assumptions or fill in the gaps yourself.

THE BIG QUESTION: As you minister to others, do you ask good, biblical questions or is your ministry weakened by assumptions?

CPR

Concepts

1. Insightful people are not the people with the right answers but the ones who ask the right questions. We cannot arrive at the right answers without the right questions.

2. Christ is our example of entering a person's world, understanding what is there, and thus being able to fully sympathize and understand.

3. Relationships that are trapped in the casual don't lend themselves to fruitful personal ministry.

Personalized

1. I need to be interested in the lives of the people around me if I want opportunities to serve as an instrument of change.

2. I need to be committed to move beyond the casual at home, at work, in my neighborhood, and in the body of Christ.

3. I need to ask where I have missed ministry opportunities that God has given me because I did not know the person well enough to understand and respond.

Related to others

1. I need to be committed to asking good questions of people, not to satisfy my curiosity but to fulfill my call as one of Christ's ambassadors.

2. I need to ask what I do not know about people that keeps me from effective personal ministry.

3. I want to be a sympathetic and understanding instrument in God's hands, one to whom people can come with confidence.

Make It Real

Reflect on your Personal Ministry Opportunity in the following ways:

1. List the places where you have been tempted to make assumptions instead of asking questions you needed to ask.

2. Where do you have gaps in your information about this person/ group and his/their world?

3. List some open-ended questions you could ask to get this information.

4. Pray for God's wisdom and discernment as you seek to understand this person or group.

Know II: Getting to Know People; Discovering Where Change Is Needed

DISCUSS HOMEWORK

REVIEW

Jina is an attractive seventeen-year-old high school student who has always done well in school. Recently she has refused to get out of bed in the mornings and protested about going to school. She is spending an unusual amount of time in her room. Last night she sat through dinner with her head down. When her mother asked her what was wrong, she said she was too depressed to eat and ran out of the room. At that point, her mother called you.

- What open-ended questions would you ask?
- What survey questions would you ask?

- What focused questions would you ask?
- What different kinds of questions would you ask to uncover different kinds of information?
- Ask a progressive line of questions in which each question is based on information from the previous question.

CONCEPTS AND OBJECTIVES

Concept: Personal ministry is not shaped by the facts you gather but by the way you interpret those facts.

Personalized: I need to think in distinctively biblical ways about myself and the people God places in my path.

Related to others: One of the primary ways to function as an instrument of change is to help others think biblically about their situations and relationships, thoughts, motives, and behavior.

LESSON CONTENT

Have you ever had someone ask for your help with a problem, and you simply didn't know what to say? Has someone ever asked you, "What does the Bible say about 'x'?" and you didn't have an answer? Do you know that you never respond to life based on the facts of your experiences but on your interpretation of those facts? Do you know that as you listen to others share their story you are instinctively and actively making sense out of what you are hearing? Do you know that whatever you say in response will not be based on what they said but on the sense that you made out of it?

Because we are always interpreting and because we have been called to be Christ's ambassadors, it is essential that we learn how to make biblical sense out of our lives and the lives of those around us. Only in this way can we know someone as God intends.

The Blind Leading the Blind

Have you ever noticed that we may spend hours preparing for a Sunday school class, a Bible study, or an elders' meeting, yet we will offer counsel to someone on the spur of the moment, with little or no preparation?

For example, your friend calls you in great distress. She was cleaning out her son's sock drawer and found a bag of marijuana. Without missing a beat, you begin to advise her on how to handle this very serious issue. Because we do not take the time to think biblically about what others share with us, very often we are the blind leading the blind.

As we seek to know and help people, we must always ask ourselves, "What principles, promises, perspectives, themes, and commands of Scripture speak to this person in this situation?" Our counsel will only be biblical if we have taken time to filter what we have heard through a sound biblical grid.

There is never a day when we do not advise and counsel one another. A wife may advise her husband as he is getting ready for work. A parent may coach a child on how to face a difficulty at school. A brother may help his sister talk through some problems with her friends. A boss may confront a worker.

It may involve nothing more than what to order at the local diner, or it may be a serious discussion over the future of a marriage. But every day we influence one another. Every day we share our interpretations of life with one another and tell people what we think about their circumstances, relationships, and responses.

The question is whether our "ministry" to one another is biblical. In all of this talk, are we asking ourselves what the Bible has to say about what we are discussing? If not, it is very easy for all of that advice-giving to be little more than the blind leading the blind.

Organizing the Information Biblically

Getting to know other people is like going around the house and collecting the laundry. Before long, we will have gathered a diverse pile of clothes, but they all must be sorted before we throw them in the washer!

The same is true of getting to know other people. We don't talk about ourselves in organized categories. What we say comes out in a messy and chaotic way. We mix past history with present circumstances. We mix emotions right in with logical thoughts. We interpret the behavior of others when we talk about ourselves. We say things about God as we describe our circumstances. It all comes out as a messy pile of facts that need organization and interpretation.

One way to promote godly change in others is to learn how to think about what they say in an organized, biblical way. We can then help them interpret their lives and make changes that reflect God's truth. This lesson will teach you how to do that.

Let's say that John's wife Greta asks to talk with you. When you meet, she says that she is concerned about her husband. John has an increasingly short fuse. He yells at her and the children at the drop of a hat. He is critical and demanding. He is spending more time at work, and most of his home time is spent on the computer.

When Greta asks John what is wrong, he just says that life stinks. Greta says that John's dad was a negative guy who always thought that people were out to get him. John was not like that when she married him, but Greta is afraid he is turning into his father. When Greta asks John how she can help him, all he says is, "Just give me a little space so I can breathe."

Now look at figure 8-1. This is a simple tool to help you sort the information you receive as you get to know someone. Ask yourself the four questions to organize what he tells you.

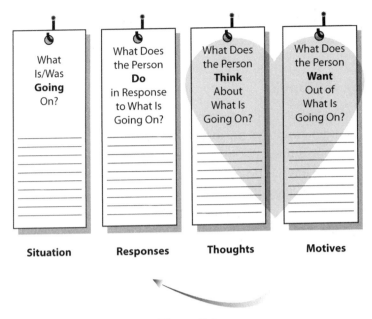

Figure 8-1.
Knowing a Person Biblically

1. *The Situation.* (What is going on?) Here you place all the information that describes what the person's world is like. You must include both past and present. (In the past, John was raised by a negative, cynical father. In the present, he is an increasingly angry, critical, and distant husband.)

2. *The Responses.* (What does the person do in response to what is going on?) Here you include facts that describe the person's behavior. (John is yelling at his family, spending more time at work, and staying on the computer at home.)

3. *The Thoughts.* (What does the person think about what is going on?) Include information on how he has been interpreting his world. ("Life stinks.")

4. *The Motives.* (What does the person want out of, or in the midst of, what is going on?) Include what you know about the person's desires, goals, purposes, treasures, motives, values, and idols. What does he live for? What really rules his heart? ("Just give me space so I can breathe.")

These four categories (Situation, Responses, Thoughts, Motives), provide four hooks to organize the information gathered.

Using the Hooks

1. *The Situation.* For personal ministry to be effective, you must understand the person's everyday world. What pressures, opportunities, responsibilities, and temptations does she face every day? Who are the significant people in her life, and what are they doing? What circumstances does she face every day? What is known about her past (the people and circumstances then)? From all this information you want to extract the things that will help you understand her world. So ask, "What is (was) going on?" Hang all of the situational information on this hook.

To sort out what you learn about someone's past history and present situation, you can use the following two lists of questions. They are not meant to be exhaustive lists but "pump-primers" to give you a sense of the kinds of things to listen for.

Historical

- Family of origin. What do you know about this person's childhood?
- Dynamic events. What major events (death in the family, divorce, crippling accident, etc.) shaped or influenced this person's life?
- Significant relationships. Outside the home, who were the people of influence in this person's life (coach, relative, friend, teacher, pastor, etc.)?
- Significant experiences. These are not the crisis events but the long-term experiences that shaped the person's life (major family move, going to college, coming to Christ).

Remember, this list is not exhaustive. It simply suggests things that may be important to understand about the person's past.

Present

- The life context. These are all the situations and relationships that the person faces every day (pressures, opportunities, responsibilities, temptations, etc.).
- Significant relationships. Who are the people of influence in this person's life today?
- Present family. What have you learned about the family in which this person is currently living?
- Presenting problem. How does the person describe her struggle? What does she say is wrong?

The goal here is to get to know this person in her world. You need to know the details of her world because your call, as Christ's ambassador, is to represent him (in his message, methods, character) in that context. Your calling is to build a bridge of understanding from the Word of God to the details of her world so that she can understand what God has promised her and called her to do. So, you begin by pulling out of your pile of information everything you have learned about this person's situation. You place it under the question, "What is going on?"

2. *The Responses.* Here the focus is on the person's behavior. You know she has been acting, reacting, and responding. You want to collect all the information that describes what this person does in response to what is going on in her world.

   As you do this, you look for themes and patterns. What are the typical ways she responds to situations and people? These themes and patterns will give you some idea of what is going on in her heart. (Certain roots in the heart produce certain fruit in the person's life.) So, you take out any information that describes this person's behavior and place it under the question, "What does this person do in response to what is going on?"

3. *The Thoughts.* Here you are considering the "heart" that directs the person's behavior. You know that this person is a meaning maker; that is, she is always trying to make sense out of her life. You know that this person doesn't respond just to

the facts of her life but to her interpretation of those facts. You know that lasting change always takes place through the pathway of the heart. So, if you are going to be an instrument of change, it is vital to know how this person is thinking. There is a very real possibility that change will need to begin here.

Remember that the thoughts of the heart precede and determine our activity. Turn to Numbers 11. This passage gives us a window on the importance of our thoughts about a particular situation and how those thoughts shape our responses.

Israel is in the wilderness and God is sending manna for food. The Israelites become dissatisfied and begin craving other food. God finally responds to their complaint by sending quail, three feet deep, for as far as a person could walk in a day! Let's look at the thinking of the children of Israel as they responded to their situation.

- They had a distorted view of the *past*. The description of Egypt in verses 4 and 5 sounds more like a restaurant than a place of suffering, slavery, and death! For 420 years Israel had prayed to be liberated from this place. Now they were longing for it. Our perspective on our past is often shockingly selective.
- They had a distorted view of the *present*. The average Israelite, standing at his tent door and seeing manna morning after morning, thought of this situation as an awful trial. Yet they were experiencing one of the clearest indications of God's covenant faithfulness they had ever seen. Because he had promised to sustain them when they could not produce food themselves, God harnessed the forces of nature to provide for his people. This is such a clear demonstration of his love that Jesus takes "Manna" as one of his names. He declares that he is the bread that has come down from heaven, the only bread that can truly satisfy (John 6:32–35). The Israelites should have looked at the manna each morning and thought, *How could God love us enough to do this miraculous thing day after day?*
- They had a distorted view of *self*. Moses is our example here. His prayer in verses 10–15 reveals that he had a completely distorted perspective on who he was and what he had been

called to do. He thought it was his job to "carry" Israel. He was so convinced that he had been given an impossible job to do that he asked God to take his life! There was clear evidence in the cloud by day, the pillar of fire by night, and the manna every morning that it was God who was guiding and sustaining his people. Moses' view of himself and his job could not have been more distorted.

- They had a distorted view of *God.* Combining Israel's complaints against God with Moses' view of God (vv. 21–22) gives a picture of how distorted Israel's functional theology actually was. As Israel saw it, God was distant and uncaring. He was weak and small. He was untrustworthy. He was not a god to whom one would entrust her life and her future.

- They had a distorted view of the *future.* According to the thinking of the Israelites, what options did they have? On the one hand, they could go back to Egypt where good food was available, but where they would once again be subjected to slavery, suffering, and death. Or, they could entrust themselves to a god who was distant, uncaring, untrustworthy, and weak. This is functional hopelessness—neither situation seems attractive or workable. The future appears to give Israel no reason for hope and, because of that, no reason to continue.

If I have a distorted view of the past, present, myself, God, and the future, there is no way that I will respond properly to what God has placed on my plate. We need to look for the seeds of wrong behavior in a person's distorted and unbiblical thought. Because of this, it is vital to organize all of the facts that describe how this person thinks about life. We place all of that information under the question, "What does this person think about what is going on?"

4. *The Motives.* We know that there is always something or someone ruling our hearts. We know that whatever rules our hearts will control our behavior. We know that our desires battle for control within our hearts. We know that we all live for certain treasures. We know that behind every action, reaction, or response are desires, motives, goals, and purposes.

We know that we quickly exchange worship and service for the Creator for worship and service of the created thing.

So, it is very important to collect all the information that describes what this person truly wants, what desires really rule her heart, or what idols have taken control. Because our behavior is our attempt to get what is important to us from people and situations, real change will always include the motives of the heart. Because of this, we must be able to identify the person's motives. We place all of this information under the question, "What does this person want out of (or in the midst of) what is going on?"

Once we have organized the information the person has given us, it is no longer a chaotic pile of facts. It is now in categories that help the information to speak to us. This should help us see where change needs to take place in this person's life.

An Opportunity to Use the Tool

Below is a case study about "Sharon." Let's attempt to use the hook illustration to organize the information given.

SHARON

Sharon approached me after our Sunday service. She said that her marriage was a "mess" and that we needed to talk "immediately." I told her that it sounded too important to squeeze into a few minutes. I set a time to meet with Sharon and asked her to invite her husband. Sharon came alone and told her story emotionally and in great detail. She said that her husband Ed was unwilling to come. He told her that either she "got her act together" or he was "out of here."

Sharon told of an increasingly tense relationship. She spoke of the fact that she and Ed were no longer sleeping in the same room or going anywhere together. They had separate bank accounts and recently had agreed it was "best" to eat supper separately. Their two young children took turns eating with each parent.

Even before their marriage they had experienced problems in communication. Ed felt that Sharon was always trying to control him and his decisions. Sharon felt that Ed never really paid attention to her viewpoint unless she "made it real clear." Yet Ed always said that Sharon was the most beautiful woman in the world, and Sharon said that Ed was the best thing that had ever happened to her.

Ed was a "mover and shaker" with an ever-expanding import business, and Sharon enjoyed being with "people that matter." Sharon had lived in foster homes all her life, never truly knowing her real parents. Ed was raised in a typical working class neighborhood in the city.

Sharon said that Ed had been saying for years that she was slowly destroying his manhood. Sharon confessed to having two affairs during the marriage. She said that Ed was very angry, and she appeared to be the same.

Sharon made her agenda for counseling very clear when we first talked by saying, "I am not here to work on me. I think I am okay. I am here because my marriage is in trouble. Do you think you can get my husband to talk to you? He's the one who needs help!"

THE BIG QUESTION: In personal ministry, do you take time to organize information in a way that helps you interpret it biblically?

CPR

Concepts
1. Personal ministry is not shaped by the facts you gather but by the way you interpret those facts.

2. Interpreting information biblically begins with organizing the material under biblical categories.

Personalized

1. I need to be aware that I never live based on the facts of my experience but on how I interpret those facts.

2. Because I am always interpreting, I need to be aware of how my reactions to others are shaped by the sense I have made out of their choices, behavior, and words.

3. I must be committed to making Scripture my primary tool for interpreting life.

Related to others

1. One of the primary ways I will function as God's instrument of change is to help those around me to think about their lives in a distinctively biblical way.

2. As I get to know people, I need to take the time necessary to let biblical categories sort out the information they give me.

3. As I listen to people tell their stories, I need to ask, "What does the Bible say about what I am hearing?"

Make It Real

In light of your Personal Ministry Opportunity, use the following categories and questions to organize the information you have gathered about your person or group. Refer to the Sharon case study as an example.

1. *Situation.* List everything you can find about the person's circumstances.

2. *Response.* List everything you can that characterizes the person's responses to circumstances.

3. *Thoughts.* List everything you can that describes the way the person thinks about his situation. How is he thinking about himself, God, change, and so forth?

4. *Motives.* List everything you can that describes what the person wants out of (or in the midst of) the situation.

5. Pray specifically for God's wisdom and discernment as you try to understand this person.

LESSON 9

Speak I: Speaking the Truth in Love

DISCUSS HOMEWORK

REVIEW

CONCEPTS AND OBJECTIVES

Concepts: Confrontation needs to be rooted in the comfort and call of the gospel.

Personalized: I must examine my life. Do the promises, provisions, and obligations of the gospel shape my living?

Related to others: As I seek to help others examine themselves in the mirror of God's Word, I must be committed to encouraging and comforting them with the gospel.

LESSON CONTENT

Rebuke is the word the Bible uses for bringing truth to where change is needed, yet most of us don't have positive reactions when we hear this word. For example, if I called you one night and told you that I would like to come over the next morning to rebuke you, how would you respond? Would you run to your friend and say, "The most wonderful thing is going to happen to me tomorrow! _____ is coming over to rebuke me. It has been so long since I've been rebuked. I just can't wait!" It's not likely that this would be your reaction.

When we think of rebuke, we often think of a tense moment, of harsh words, red faces, ultimatums, and threats. We don't think of something that is an act of patient and committed love. So it is important for us to consider what a biblical model of rebuke looks like. We need to know what "speaking the truth in love" is all about. This is the focus of this lesson.

The Process of Confrontation

As we consider bringing truth to where change is needed, perhaps the best way to begin is to talk about our goals, the results that should motivate us when we speak. Second Corinthians 5:20 is very helpful here. It reminds us that we must approach truth-speaking in personal ministry as God's representatives. What should motivate us is not our opinion, our anger, or our impatience. What should motivate us is God's desire to make his appeal to that person through us!

Think about that for a moment. Almighty God has actually chosen to say important, life-changing things through us! In moments of biblical rebuke, our opinion doesn't make any difference. The only thing that counts is God's perspective as revealed in his Word. As God's representative, we must be careful not to combine what God has said with what we've always wanted to say.

In a rebuke, we want to incarnate the love of Christ by helping people to see themselves in the mirror of God's Word and calling them to accept responsibility for sins of their heart and behavior.

If we have this as our goal, the process will look like the following:

1. *Start with ourselves.* If we are going to speak as ambassadors, we affirm that biblical truth-speaking always begins with dealing with our own hearts. We need to confess and forsake all the wrong thoughts and motives (anger, bitterness, thoughts of vengeance, a spirit of condemnation, etc.) that would stand in the way of what the Lord wants to do through us. And we must ask God to provide the love, courage, patience, and wisdom that we will need to represent him well. This step of personal preparation is often neglected in moments of confrontation. The result is that the rebuke is not effective, not only because the receiver was unwilling but also because the representative was unprepared. If we do not start with our own hearts we will tend to:

- Turn moments of ministry into moments of anger
- Personalize things that are not personal
- Be adversarial in our approach
- Confuse our opinions with God's will
- Settle for quick solutions that do not address the heart

2. *Understand why people need to be confronted.* After our personal preparation, we can consider the goals we should have in view. The best way to do this is to ask the question, "Why do people need to

be confronted?" The answers will direct us toward the proper set of goals. People need to be confronted because of:

- The deceitfulness of sin, which blinds our hearts (Hebrews 3:12–13)
- Wrong and unbiblical thinking (Numbers 11; Psalm 73).
- Emotional thinking (we are all aware that we don't do our best thinking in times of great emotion; we will often be ministering to people who are in the midst of situations that are emotionally volatile)
- Our view of life (God, self, others, the solution, etc.) tends to be strengthened by our experiences. Because we are the one interpreting our experiences, our conclusions tend to be reinforced with each new situation. What we need is an intervention of truth to confront and correct our thinking.

3. *Speak with God's goals in view.* Our goals for rebuke must be equal to these challenges. Two goals together meet the standard.

The first is that in confrontation, we would be used as God's instruments of seeing in the life of another. Yes, we do tend to be blind, and we do tend to be more aware of where others need to change and grow than we are of ourselves. So the goal of truth-speaking is to help people clearly see themselves in the mirror of God's Word. We are not there to help them see what we see but what God sees. Because of this, it is the Word of God, and not our personal opinions, that we will hold before them.

The second goal of confrontation is to be used of God as an agent of repentance. The biblical definition of repentance is a change of heart that leads to a change in the direction of our lives. True repentance always begins with the heart.

Turn to Joel 2:12–13, which captures this for us.

Joel talks not of rending the garments (the external behavior of remorse) but of rending the heart (heartfelt remorse for our sin accompanied by a desire to change). This is our goal, not to pressure and coerce people into changes in behavior but to encourage heart change that impacts the person's response to life. Repentance literally means to turn and go in the other direction. This turning must begin with the heart.

So, as we try to speak truth into people's lives, we are not trying to advance our own opinions. Rather, we want to function as instruments of seeing. We are not seeking simply to coerce the people into altering their behavior. Rather, our goal is that through the things we say (message), the way we say them (methods), and the attitudes we express (character), God will change their hearts.

Don't Leave the Gospel at the Door

A mistake we often make as we seek to lead someone to repentance is to emphasize the law over the gospel. Yet Paul says (Romans 2:4) that it is God's kindness (goodness) that leads us to repentance. He also says (2 Corinthians 5:14) that it is the love of Christ that compels us to no longer live for ourselves but for him. It is the grace of the gospel that turns our hearts because the gospel is God's magnificent promise of forgiveness in Christ Jesus. This is what draws us out of hiding into the light of truth, where true confession and repentance will take place.

As we confront people, we need to remind them of their identity in Christ (2 Peter 1:3–9; 1 John 3:1–3). We need to remind them of God's promise of forgiveness (1 John 1:5–10) and the amazing gift of the indwelling Holy Spirit (Ephesians 3:20), who gives us the strength to obey. These truths give believers the courage to examine their hearts, confess their sin, and turn to Christ. If we are speaking as agents of repentance, it is not enough to come armed with the law. We must come armed with the gospel as well.

Romans 8:1–17 is helpful here because Paul captures the two sides of the gospel.

Paul begins by alerting us to the comfort of the gospel (vv. 1–11). He points to two powerful redemptive realities. First, the work of the Lord Jesus Christ has removed the sentence of condemnation that was on our heads because of our sin. Jesus paid the penalty for our sin. As we come to God in confession, we do not need to fear his wrath and rejection. Because Christ met the requirements of the law and went to the cross as an acceptable sin offering, we do not face condemnation! As we hold the mirror of the Word in front of people, helping them to see the presence and gravity of their sin, it is very important that we also comfort them with the fact that the work of Christ has satisfied God's anger. As we come to him, we can be confident that he will forgive.

The gospel also comforts us with the Holy Spirit, who lives within every believer. Before salvation, we were controlled by the thoughts and desires of the sinful nature. We were not able to live as God has ordained. But now God lives inside us! We are no longer controlled by the sinful nature. We no longer have to live as slaves to its passions and desires. The Holy Spirit now controls us. Paul says that the Holy Spirit gives life to our mortal bodies. What does this mean? It means that we are now dead to the controlling power of sin and alive for the purpose of obedience. God lives within us. We can follow him in simple acts of obedience amid life's daily situations and relationships. We do not have to live as if we are still a slave to sin. No, the Spirit has come to give us life, power, and the desire and ability to obey.

As we call people to own and confess their need before God, we must root our loving words of confrontation in the soil of the gospel. Condemnation has been removed. Forgiveness has been granted. The Holy Spirit lives inside us. We have power to obey. These truths give people the confidence they need to come out of hiding and confess their sin. And they give people the confidence that as they turn to a new way of living, they will have God's strength to do what he calls them to do. Write down a Bible passage on forgiveness and the work of the Holy Spirit that has encouraged you.

But this is not all that Paul says about the gospel. Paul says that the gospel is not only a comfort; it is also a call. The call of the gospel is summarized by Paul in Romans 8:12–17. Paul uses the word *obligation* to define what the gospel calls us to. He essentially says that the ongoing work of God in believers' lives is to eradicate sin ("put to death the misdeeds of the body").

As believers, we are obligated to participate in the Holy Spirit's search-and-destroy mission. We must not live "according to the sinful nature" any longer. We must accept our sonship, realizing that true sons of God are those who are "led by the Spirit" and not by the sinful nature.

Here is what we are seeking to accomplish as we root our truth-speaking in the gospel. Our goal is that the heart would be changed by the work of Christ that the gospel declares. First, our goal is that the gospel promises of forgiveness and power would give people real hope of change. Second, our goal is that the call of the gospel would cause people to accept responsibility for their sin and to accept God's call to obey.

The heart that has embraced both the hope (comfort) and the obligation (call) is now ready to receive words of confrontation. Now a person can see the gravity of his sin and the grandeur of God's call to obey in light of gospel truths. He is now ready to really live as a true child of God, as someone who is honest about himself and ready to follow God in daily acts of faith and obedience.

THE BIG QUESTION: Is the gospel central when you speak the truth to someone?

CPR

Concepts
1. The purpose of confrontation is twofold: to help people see what God wants them to see and to lead them to repentance.

2. As we speak truth to people, we must not only bring the law to them but the gospel as well.

3. It is the hope of Christ's forgiveness and the promise of his presence that draws us out of hiding toward confession and repentance.

Personalized

1. I must ask myself, "Do I confront others as an ambassador, or do I tend to advance my own opinion?"

2. Am I zealous to comfort and encourage people with the gospel?

3. Is my life shaped and directed by the comfort and the call of the gospel?

Related to others

1. Do I look for opportunities to motivate people with the truths of the gospel?

2. Do I look for opportunities to function as one of God's instruments of seeing?

3. In moments of confrontation, do I want people to agree with me or turn to God?

Make It Real

In light of your Personal Ministry Opportunity, answer the following questions.

1. Think of a time in your life (1) when you were rebuked and (2) you had to rebuke someone else. How well did these encounters fulfill godly goals? Now apply this to your Personal Ministry Opportunity. Have you begun with yourself? Are you moving

toward the other person with a proper understanding of why he or she needs rebuke? Are you moving toward him with proper goals—to be an instrument of sight or an agent of repentance? Or are you going with ungodly motives: revenge, the desire to prove that you are right and he is wrong, and so on? Pray consistently for love, honesty, and humility.

2. What do you dislike most about confrontation? How can a gospel perspective, as both a comfort and a call, help you move toward the person you have chosen as your ministry focus? Where do you need compassion and courage, honesty and humility, encouragement and candor?

3. Study three of the gospel passages that your group shared during this lesson. Write down the specific comforts and provisions that they offer the child of God. How can you use them to encourage the person you need to confront?

LESSON 10

Speak II: Speaking the Truth in Love

DISCUSS HOMEWORK

REVIEW

In lesson 9 we focused on the importance of confrontation being rooted in the gospel. It is the comfort of the gospel that draws us out of hiding and brings us to the Lord with humble words of confession and obedient acts of repentance. It is the call of the gospel that causes us to be serious about sin and to faithfully participate as God works to remove it from our lives. If a person is going to be helped by the truth that is spoken to him, he must embrace both the hope and the obligation of the gospel.

We also examined the goal of confrontation. We do not speak the truth to advance our own opinions or to say things we have always wanted to say. Rather, to confront is to serve as an ambassador, communicating God's truth to someone. It is motivated by two goals:

1. To serve as an instrument of seeing in this person's life. Our hope is that our words would help this person see himself in the perfect mirror of God's Word.
2. To be an agent of true repentance (a radical change of heart that leads to a radical change in the life).

In this lesson we will examine the progressive steps of confrontation and consider what the process should look like.

CONCEPTS AND OBJECTIVES

Concept: The progressive steps of confrontation are consideration, confession, commitment, and change.

Personalized: I must be committed to a "put off" (consideration, confession) and "put on" (commitment, change) personal lifestyle.

Related to others: I must be committed to a process of speaking truth to others that encourages lasting change.

LESSON CONTENT

We all confront one another every day. A mom goes to wake her daughter for school and confronts her about the condition of her room. A brother confronts his sister, who took something from his room without permission. A wife confronts her husband about his distance and busyness. A neighbor confronts her neighbor about the way he spoke to her children. A pastor confronts a wayward man in his congregation. A driver confronts another driver in traffic. A consumer confronts a store manager about his deceptive advertising. A married child confronts his mother about her interference in his marriage. Confrontation is a much more regular part of our daily lives than we often think.

The question in the midst of all this confrontation is, *Whose agenda are we following?* Are we confronting others like mini-kings, communicating our opinion and trying to get people to do what would please us? Or are we confronting as ambassadors, helping others see themselves clearly in the mirror of God's Word, leading them to real repentance of the heart? This is the focus of this lesson. We want to examine the steps of biblical confrontation (confronting as ambassadors of Christ).

Progressive Steps of Confrontation

If we want to do more than read people a list of charges from Scripture or tell them what we think of them, we must speak the truth with a clear sense of direction. If our goal is to function as instruments of seeing and agents of repentance, there are four specific steps to the process.

Let's say that you are friends with both Sally and Jim. Sally has expressed concern to you that Jim has begun to do things that are unbecoming to a Christian. He admits to cheating on his hours at work and to taking office supplies. He has been going to clubs that Sally thinks would make any Christian uncomfortable.

Jim also reports a deteriorating relationship with his roommate, and Sally has been hurt that things she told Jim in confidence have been shared with you. She has tried to talk to Jim about his relationship with God. He has told you both that he is "discouraged with God" right now. He is thinking about changing churches or even moving away. You are concerned for Jim, know him well, and have a relationship of mutual trust. You decide to talk with him.

1. *Consideration.* The question to ask here is, "What does Jim need to see [about himself, God, others, life, truth, change, etc.] that he does not now see, and how can I help him see it?" Often when people tell their story, they are not in it! Their account focuses on the toughness of the situation and the attitudes and behavior of others. Your goal is to encourage Jim to look at his behavior and to examine his heart. You want to

break through the walls of spiritual blindness and help him to see himself, his relationships, and his circumstances with biblical eyes. To accomplish this goal, there are five questions that you should regularly ask. The order is important because it teaches you to think biblically about why you do the things you do.

- *What was going on?* This question gives Jim an opportunity to tell what was happening around him. This information is important for him because you want him to see that these things did not cause him to do what he did. It is important for you because you need to understand his world in order to speak truth into it. Do not assume that you know the details of any person's situation!

- *What were you thinking and feeling as it was going on?* This question immediately directs Jim to examine his heart. In asking this question, you are teaching him to be aware that the heart is always interacting with what is going on. You never leave your heart at the door.

- *What did you do in response?* Again, notice the order of the questions. It reflects the fact that behavior is not shaped by the facts of situations and relationships but by your heart's response to those facts. In asking this question at this time, you are asking Jim to admit that his behavior was not forced upon him by the situation ("It was the only thing I could do!") or by others ("She made me angry!"). It was shaped by what is in his heart.

- *Why did you do it?* What were you seeking to accomplish? If the second question uncovers thoughts, then this question reveals motives. In asking this question, you are teaching Jim that the heart is always serving something. Behavior is always directed by a functional worship and service for the Creator or for the creation (Romans 1:25). Here Jim is asked to consider how his behavior is his attempt to get what is important to him. Behavior is always an expression of the purposes, desires, motives, treasures, lusts, or idols of the heart. Notice that questions 2 and 4 connect behavior to the thoughts and motives of the heart (Hebrews 4:12).

The order forces Jim to consider how his behavior is a logical expression of how his heart thinks and what his heart wants.

- *What was the result?* This question not only seeks to uncover consequences (Galatians 6:7) but the way these consequences are a direct result of the thoughts and motives of the heart. The seeds planted in the heart grow into a full harvest of fruit in Jim's situations and relationships. (We are all quite skilled at denying our own harvest—"If you had these kids, you'd yell too!" "I didn't really hear what you said." "He just pushes my buttons!") So it is important to get Jim to examine the fruit in his life in terms of his heart. You want to lead Jim to "own" his own harvest. This happens when Jim is willing to look at himself in the only mirror that is truly accurate, the Word of God.

2. *Confession.* This is the next logical step in the process. If Jim has looked at himself in the mirror of Scripture, he should have identified sins of heart and behavior that need to be confessed. The problem is that we sinners find confession difficult. It is more natural for us to deny, recast history, explain away, accuse, blame, defend, and hide. Jim's confession needs to be concrete and specific and not weakened by "if onlys." It is equally important that you do not confess for Jim but that you lead him to speak his own words of confession to the Lord. Further, he needs to be encouraged to confess horizontally, that is, to all of the people who have been affected by his sin.

   Don't assume confession! At appropriate times call the person to confession; ask him to pray, admit his sin, and seek God's forgiveness.

3. *Commitment.* The question to ask here is, "Specifically, where is God calling Jim to radical new ways of living?" To what new ways of thinking is God calling him? What new biblical desires would God want to control his heart? To what new responses is God calling him? In what new ways is God calling him to serve and love others? What things should he stop doing? What new things should he start doing? What steps of

correction and restitution is God calling him to make? What new habits need to be inserted into his daily routine? Is Jim committed to these things?

4. *Change.* It is easy to assume that change has taken place because Jim has gained personal insight and made new commitments, but that would be a mistake. Change hasn't taken place until change has taken place! Daily Jim needs to apply the insights and commitments in his life circumstances and relationships. Commitment is the "what," and change is the "how."

How will a husband begin to express servant love for his wife when he comes home from work? How will a son demonstrate a new honor and respect for his parents? In what ways can a man serve instead of control? How will a woman go about restoring a broken relationship? How will a man make changes in his slavery to his career? What new habits will a distant father insert into his daily routine so that he can more faithfully and lovingly parent his children? Change involves applying new commitments to the situations and relationships of daily living.

If we want our words to be instruments of change in moments of confrontation, we need a sense of direction. These four steps provide a road map for us:

1. *Consideration.* What does God want the person to see?
2. *Confession.* What does God want the person to admit and confess?
3. *Commitment.* To what new ways of living is God calling this person?
4. *Change.* How should these new commitments be applied to daily living?

Learn to Confront Biblically

We need to get away from a reading-the-person-the-riot-act style of confrontation. In this style, the receiver is essentially silent while the confronter lays out a list of "charges" and calls for a response.

In Scripture, the more common style of confrontation is interaction. The confronter stands alongside the person, helping him to see, telling stories, asking questions, drawing out answers, and then calling for a response. The confrontation has much more of a conversational structure.

The primary example of this kind of confrontation is Christ and his parables. (See Luke 7:36–50; 14:1–14.) Christ speaks so that people might see, and in seeing, might confess, and in confessing, might turn. He confronts powerful attitudes, beliefs, and actions, yet the parables have a very different feel from our often tense moments of confrontation.

The principle here is, *Start with interaction*. Interactive confrontation includes:

- *Two-way communication.* If you want to be an instrument of seeing, the person being confronted must be invited to talk. You need to know that she has seen and understood what you are pointing out; that she has owned what needs to be admitted and confessed; that she is committed to new ways of living; and that she understands how change needs to be made. Feedback is vital.
- *Use of metaphor* (example: God is a rock, fortress, sun, shield, door, light, etc.). Here you are searching for things in a person's life that illustrate truth. (Reflect on the ministry of Christ and his use of common things to communicate uncommon truths.)

    What do you know about this person's background, job, interests, experiences, and so forth, that would provide metaphors for you to use? The metaphor can be a single comparison ("He is a whirlwind") or an extended story (the parables of Christ).
- *Self-confronting statements.* Here you are encouraging the person to make connections between the examples you have used and his own life. Don't rush to make those connections for him! It is vital that his heart embraces what God is showing him and that, without pressure, he is ready to confess and turn from sin.

- *Summary.* Here you are drawing together all that you think God wants to teach the person and calling him to respond with heartfelt commitment. When you summarize, make sure that the issues are clear and that you don't assume a person's agreement. Ask for commitment.

In moments of confrontation, it is always important to start with interaction. But there are times when we are called to minister to individuals who are stubborn, rebellious, and proud. Such people (the Pharisees, for example) will not participate in the give-and-take of interactive confrontation. They need to hear God's will pronounced and be exhorted to respond. This style of confrontation, declaration, is what we most often associate with confrontation, but it should be reserved for those who refuse to do the self-examination that interactive confrontation requires.

We should always begin with interaction (engaging a person in heartfelt self-examination) and only move to declaration ("Thus says the Lord," with a call to repent) when interaction is ineffective. (See 2 Samuel 12:1–14; Amos 6; Matthew 23:13–39).

THE BIG QUESTION: What does it look like to confront someone biblically?

CPR

Concepts

1. The goal of confrontation is lasting change in a person's heart and life.

2. The progressive steps of confrontation are: consideration, confession, commitment, and change.

3. If the goals of confrontation are to help a person see his sin and repent, then it is essential that the confrontation be interactive.

Personalized

1. I must be committed to a process of truth-speaking that results in lasting heart change.

2. I must follow the example of Christ as I speak truth and seek to give sight to those around me.

3. I must ask myself, Where is God seeking to help me see and lead me to repentance?

Related to others

1. I must patiently lead people through the steps of confrontation.

2. I must learn to ask good, heart-revealing questions.

3. I must learn to find metaphors in others' lives that help them to see truth.

Make It Real

Answer the following questions in light of your Personal Ministry Opportunity.

1. How will the progressive steps of confrontation help your confrontation to be godly?

a. What does the person need to consider? How will you help him see what he needs to see?

b. What things does he need to confess? How will you assist him in godly confession?

c. What commitments does the person need to make? How can you help them be specific and concrete?

d. What practical changes need to take place? How will you assist the person to be specific so that he can determine whether real change has happened?

2. How will you best confront the person you have chosen for your Personal Ministry Opportunity? Be creative as you study the multiple ways that confrontation can take place: two-way communication, use of metaphor, self-confrontation, summary.

3. How well have you done the confrontation described in questions 1 and 2? What have you typically done? Where do you need to change? Do you need to confess sinful and unwise behavior to the person you have chosen for your Personal Ministry Opportunity?

4. Pray honestly and faithfully for God's work in your heart in these areas.

LESSON 11

Do I: Applying Change to Everyday Life

DISCUSS HOMEWORK

REVIEW

In lesson 1 we learned that:
> To be human is to need truth outside of ourselves in order to make sense out of life.

In lesson 2 we learned that:
> Whatever rules the heart will exercise inescapable influence over the life and behavior.

In lesson 3 we learned that:
> We have been united with Christ and indwelt by the Holy Spirit so that we can say no to the passions and desires of the sinful nature.

In lesson 4 we learned that:
> God has called us to be his ambassadors, faithfully representing his message, methods, and character (Love, Know, Speak, Do).

In lesson 5 we learned that:

> We must seek to build loving relationships in which the work of God can thrive.

In lesson 6 we learned that:

> God calls us to suffer so that we will be qualified agents of his comfort and compassion.

In lesson 7 we learned that:

> We need to ask questions that move us beyond the casual and help us to know when a person needs ministry.

In lesson 8 we learned that:

> We function as God's instruments of change by helping others think biblically about their situations and relationships, thoughts and motives, and behavior.

In lesson 9 we learned that:

> Confrontation must always be rooted in the comfort and call of the gospel.

In lesson 10 we learned that:

> To confront means to lead people to consider, confess, commit, and change.

In the last two lessons we will consider the final element of our personal ministry model: Do. We will learn how to apply the insights we learn and the commitments we make to everyday life.

CONCEPTS AND OBJECTIVES

Concept: To help someone change, I must have a biblical agenda for change that reflects biblical commands, principles, promises, and priorities.

Personalized: I must always ask, "What are God's goals for change in me as I face relationships and situations?"

Related to Others: In personal ministry, I must always ask, "How can I support this person in the process of change?"

LESSON CONTENT

Have you ever been encouraged by another person's promises only to have him fail to follow through? Have you ever had personal insights that did not lead to lasting change in your life? Have you ever made commitments that somehow got lost in life's frenetic pace?

Have you ever known that certain changes needed to take place, but you didn't know how to make them? Have you ever been confused as you tried to decide what things in your life were your responsibility and what things you could rightfully entrust to God? Have you ever benefited from someone holding you accountable? Have you ever felt that the changes that you need to make in your life are just impossible? These things will be our focus in the last two lessons.

Do teaches us how to carefully apply the truths we have learned, the personal insights we have gained, and the commitments we have made to the situations and relationships of daily living.

To do this, the following four things are essential:

1. *Establishing your personal ministry agenda.* This gives you a sense of direction as you minister to another.
2. *Clarifying responsibility.* As people seek to apply truths to life, the issue of who is responsible for what will always come up.
3. *Instilling identity in Christ.* Because change is a difficult process, it is important to remind people of the amazing resources that are theirs as children of God.
4. *Providing accountability.* Because change demands perseverance, we all need the encouragement, insight, and warning that a system of oversight will provide.

1. Establish Personal Ministry Agenda

It is hard to lead a person to change if we aren't sure where he should be going! Take time to establish the agenda. Does this sound too technical or formal for person-to-person ministry?

Let's begin by defining our terms. An agenda is simply a plan for accomplishing a goal. It is nothing more than a map that shows us our destination (the changes that need to take place) and how to get there (the How? Where? When? With whom? that we must consider as we institute change).

Because our goal is more than denouncing sin, and because we really do want to be God's instruments of lasting change, it is vital to know exactly where we are going and what we need to do to get there. This is where personal ministry becomes very practical, concrete, and specific: God is calling *this* person in *this* situation to *these* specific changes.

All too often, our personal ministry is at its weakest here. We will prepare for hours to teach a Sunday school class, but we will give someone very serious life advice on the spur of the moment, essentially out of our back pockets! Surely, the result is that much of our "ministry" to one another is not well thought out and therefore not solidly biblical. When we do not step back to establish a biblical sense of direction (agenda), our ministry is weakened by:

- Personal bias
- Ignorance
- Poor theology
- Misunderstanding of Scripture
- Improper application of Scripture
- Fear of man
- Emotional thinking
- Pressure of the moment

We should not speak to serious life issues impulsively and without preparation. We must step back and ask questions that will help us think clearly about God's goals for change for this person in this situation, and how to accomplish those goals. Let's consider three agenda-setting questions.

1. *What does the Bible say about the information that has been gathered?* We need to filter everything learned about this person through the grid of sound biblical thinking. (Refer to figure 8-1 as a method.) This protects our ministry from personal bias and unbiblical thinking. It enables us to speak as ambassadors, communicating clearly the message of the King.

2. *What are God's goals for change for this person in this situation?* Here we are applying God's call to put off and to put on (Ephesians 4:22–24) to the specifics of this person's thoughts, motives, and behavior. In this situation, what does God want him to think, desire, and do? In asking this question, we mark out our destination. We can't lead a person if we do not know where we are going, and in personal ministry we must only lead people where God is calling them to go.

3. *What are biblical methods for accomplishing God's goals for change?* This is the *how* of the change process. After clearly and specifically establishing biblical goals, we need to determine the best biblical means of accomplishing them. Often people will have a sense of what is wrong, but the way they seek to correct it complicates matters further. Let's say that you are ministering to a husband who confesses that he has not encouraged his wife as he should. It would not be biblical to advise him to bombard his wife with flattering words that are insincere. Nor would you advise a family in debt to have the husband work ninety hours a week! Biblical change is not only about the what; it must also include the *how*. To counsel wisely, you must know God's Word well, the situation well, and the person's heart motives well.

It is at this point that God will often surprise us. When our neighbor is mistreating us, it is not our first reaction to look for ways of doing good to him! When someone is angry with us, we don't tend to think that a soft answer will be part of the solution. The Bible not only lays out for us a surprising description of what is wrong with us but also a surprising agenda for correction. How must this person put off what needs to be put off? How must this person put on what needs to be put on? For this person in this situation, what are the concrete steps of correction to which God is calling him?

2. Clarify Responsibility

One of the most important questions in life and therefore in personal ministry is: Who is responsible for what? As we function as God's instruments of change, we will encounter people who tend to be *irresponsible.* These people fail to shoulder the responsibilities to which God has clearly called them. We will also encounter those who are *overly responsible.* These people tend to take as their responsibility things that God has not called or enabled them to do.

The third class of people we will encounter is probably the biggest of the three. These are people who are *genuinely confused* when it comes to the issue of responsibility. They are not sure which things are their God-given jobs and which things they can entrust to him. Sometimes they are mini-messiahs, trying to do things that only God can do. Sometimes they ask God to do for them what he has clearly called them to do. All of the people mentioned here need a clear understanding of their responsibility as they seek to apply change to the specifics of daily life.

Figure 11-1 is a very simple tool for biblically clarifying responsibility. Let's work through the illustration together.

Let's start with the inner oval. This oval represents a particular person's biblical job description. These are the things that God, in his Word, calls this person to do in the midst of his present situation and relationships. He needs to have a clear sense of what God calls him to do as a husband, father, neighbor, relative, son, worker, and member of the body of Christ. Here we are calling the person to biblical discipleship, that is, to deny himself, take up his cross, and follow Christ (Luke 9:23–25). Here we are calling him to no longer live for himself but for the Lord (2 Corinthians 5:14–15). Most importantly, we are making that call to discipleship clear and concrete.

In this oval, we want the person to list what he thinks are his God-assigned duties in his relationships and situation. Then we want to examine his list in the light of Scripture, asking whether these things really are what God has called him to do.

The outer oval represents those things that are important to a person (the love of a spouse, a child's salvation, etc.), yet they are beyond her ability to bring about. Therefore, they are not her responsibility. Here we are calling a person to recognize her limits and to remember God, who is faithful to his promises (Psalm 145:13) and sovereign over all things (Acts 17:24–28).

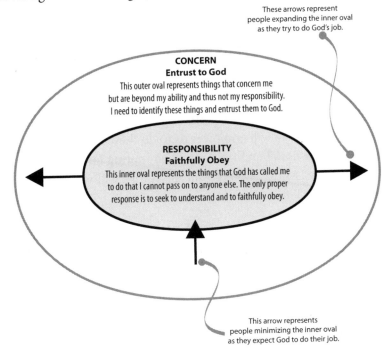

Figure 11-1.
Clarifying Responsibility

It is very important to help the person see when she has allowed the inner oval to expand into the outer one. In so doing, we are helping the person confess to where she has functioned as a mini-messiah, trying to do what only God can do. We also want to help the person to recognize and confess where she has tended to shrink the inner oval. In so doing, we are helping the person to identify places where she has, under the guise of trusting God, failed to do what God has called her to do.

Living as a mini-messiah (with too large an inner oval) has a two-sided negative effect. If we are trying to do God's job, we will experience discouragement, frustration, and failure. We will also tend to leave undone the jobs that God, in his Word, has clearly assigned to us.

For example, Alicia is concerned about her teenaged son, who is rebellious, irresponsible, unkind, and selfish. He is missing more school than he is attending. Alicia has told her friends that her goal is to "turn Matt into a responsible Christian human being if it is the last thing I ever do." This is the goal of a mini-messiah.

Attempting to give back to God what he has called us to do (too small an inner oval) will have a two-sided negative result as well. We will waste time and prayer if we wait for God to do something he has assigned us to do. He will empower us to do these things, but he will not do them for us. Therefore, we will be waiting for something we will not receive. And as we are waiting, things will worsen because of what we have left undone.

This is Sam's situation. He knows he has a broken relationship with Joe because of unkind things Sam said to him in public. Sam says he has "dealt with it in his heart" and is now waiting for God to restore the relationship. His inner oval is too small.

The Christian life is really a "trust and obey" lifestyle. We must always trust those things that are out of our control to God, and we must always be faithful to obey his clear and specific commands. Romans 12:14–21 lays out this lifestyle for us in the context of mistreatment. God clearly explains our duty in the face of mistreatment:

- Bless those who persecute you (v. 14).
- Commit to living in harmony (v. 16).
- Do not be proud (v. 16).
- As far as you can, live at peace with everyone (v. 19).
- Meet your enemy's needs (v. 20).
- Overcome evil with good (v. 21).

Paul makes it clear that in moments of mistreatment, there are things that we must not take as our responsibility. Instead, we must entrust them to God. For example, we must not retaliate or seek revenge. These are things that by their very nature only God has the right and the power to do. They are things he has promised to do. We must not load them on our shoulders. So, God says, "Vengeance and repayment belong to me. You stay out of my way ('leave room for God's wrath') and let me handle it." So we must, in a spirit of joyful submission, do what God has called us to do, and in a spirit of humble trust, give to God what he alone can do.

There are few areas more confusing than the area of personal responsibility. People need practical clarity to help them through the process of change. It is a vital part of our ministry to the people we are called to help.

THE BIG QUESTION: Do you minister to others with a clear sense of biblical direction and help them clarify their responsibilities before God?

CPR

Concepts

1. The personal ministry process is not over at the point of insight. The insights that God has given a person must be applied to the situations and relationships of his or her daily life.

2. To help a person change, we must have a biblical sense of direction (agenda) that reflects God's commands, principles, promises, and priorities.

3. One of the most important ways of functioning as an instrument of change is to help a person clarify responsibility.

Personalized

1. I must determine whether I am applying the insights that God gives me to the specifics of my daily life.

2. I must ask myself, "Are there places where I am trying to do God's job and therefore failing to do what he has called me to do?"

3. In my own life, am I confusing personal insight with concrete biblical change?

Related to others

1. Am I looking for God-given opportunities to encourage others to entrust to God those things that are out of their control?

2. Am I helping people to arrive at a clear biblical job description for their relationships and life situations?

3. Do I take time to establish a sense of direction in personal ministry so I can guide people to where God wants them to be?

Make It Real

As you continue to examine the ministry relationship(s) you have chosen to work on in your Personal Ministry Opportunity, answer the following questions.

1. What portions of Scripture help you to understand this person (or group), his situation, and his struggle in response to it?

2. What are God's goals for change for this person (or this group)?

3. How might you be part of encouraging this change? Pray regularly about this.

4. Where has the person (or group) tended to do God's job? (two circles)

5. Where has the person (or group) tended to wait for God to do what he has called him (or them) to do?

6. Have you clarified this issue of responsibility for him (or them)?

7. Where in your ministry to this person (or group) have you tended to be irresponsible, overly responsible, or confused?

LESSON 12

Do II: Applying Change to Everyday Life

DISCUSS HOMEWORK

REVIEW

Truth #1: Above all, we need God and his truth to live as we were created to live (Genesis 1:26ff; 2 Timothy 3:16–17). *Lesson 1.*

Truth #2: Each of us is called by God to be his instrument of change in the lives of others, beginning with our families and the body of Christ (Ephesians 4:11–17; Colossians 3:15–17). *Lesson 1.*

Truth #3: Our behavior is rooted in the thoughts and motives of our hearts. People and situations only prompt our hearts to express themselves in words and actions (Proverbs 4:23; Matthew 23:25; Mark 7:21; Luke 6:43–45; James 4:1–10). *Lessons 2–3.*

Truth #4: Christ has called us to be his ambassadors, following his message, methods, and character (2 Corinthians 5:14–21). *Lesson 4.*

Truth #5: Being an instrument of change means incarnating the love of Christ by sharing in people's struggles, identifying with their suffering, and extending God's grace as we call them to change (2 Corinthians 1:3–11; Colossians 3:12–14; Titus 2:11–3:8; Hebrews 2:10–11). *Lessons 5–6.*

Truth #6: Being an instrument of change means seeking to know people by guarding against false assumptions, asking good questions, and interpreting in a way that is distinctly biblical (Proverbs 20:5; Hebrews 4:14–16). *Lessons 7–8.*

Truth #7: Being an instrument of change means speaking the truth in love. With the gospel as comfort and call, we can help people to see themselves in God's Word and lead them to repentance (Romans 8:1–17; Galatians 6:1–2; James 1:22–25). *Lessons 9–10.*

Truth #8: Being an instrument of change means helping people do what God calls them to do by clarifying responsibility, offering loving accountability, and reminding them of their identity in Christ (Galatians 6:2; Philippians 2:1–14; 2 Peter 1:3–9; 1 John 3:1–3). *Lessons 11–12.*

CONCEPTS AND OBJECTIVES

Concept: Human beings always live out of some sense of identity. It is vital for the believer to understand his identity in Christ.

Personalized: I must always ask myself, "Do I view my life and myself from the vantage point of who I am in Christ?"

Related to others: Do I seek to provide encouragement and accountability to those who are following God's call to change?

LESSON CONTENT

Does it ever seem that the job God has assigned you is impossible? Are you ever overwhelmed by your responsibilities? Do you ever feel weak and unprepared? Do you encounter situations where you lack practical wisdom? Have you ever found yourself failing at the same thing over and over again? Have you ever been discouraged at the height of God's standards? Have you ever thought it would be easier if you had someone standing with you? Have you ever felt as if you were left to struggle through change all alone? Have you ever thought that you would benefit from being accountable to someone else? Have you ever sought an accountability relationship, only to find that no one was willing or available?

This lesson teaches that encouragement and accountability are very important parts of the truth application process. We were never created to live in isolation. God has designed us to live in community, first with him and then with one another. In the difficult process of change, we see our need for one another. We are not autonomous, self-sufficient beings. As we begin the process of change, we need others' encouragement and oversight.

3. Instill Identity in Christ

Human beings are always living out of some kind of identity. We are sons, daughters, bosses, employees, parents, friends, neighbors, consumers, and so forth. Our sense of identity has a powerful influence on our choices and responses. As we call people to the difficult process of change, it is important that they are living out of a gospel identity. They need to understand their position and resources as children of God.

It is easy to forget who we are as we deal with life in this fallen world, as we address age-old habits of thought, motive, and behavior, and apply new insights and commitments to daily living. This is why it is vital to keep reminding people of their identity in Christ. We want to stimulate the practical faith and courage that come from knowing who we are and what we have been given.

Peter addresses this issue in 2 Peter 1:3–9. Let's consider the important points of this passage.

- Peter proposes (v. 8) that there will be people who know the Lord but whose lives are ineffective and unproductive. These people do not produce the harvest of good fruit that we would expect from a believer.

- Peter says that these people do not produce the expected fruit of faith because they are missing essential character qualities (faith, goodness, knowledge, self-control, perseverance, godliness, brotherly kindness, and love). Because these qualities are not rooted in their hearts, they do not produce the expected fruit (vv. 5–8).
- When we see Christians who do not exhibit Christian character and are not producing good fruit, we ought to ask, "Why?" What is missing in these people? Peter says, "These people are missing character qualities that result in good fruit because they have forgotten who they are ("nearsighted and blind, and has forgotten that he has been cleansed from his past sins," v. 9). These people have lost sight of their identity in Christ, so they do not realize the position and resources that are theirs.
- Peter reminds us of one significant aspect of our identity: that in Christ we have been given "everything we need for life and godliness" (v. 3). As the children of God, we are rich! We don't just have some things. We have all that we need!

   Notice the tense of the verb in verse 3. Peter says that everything "has been given." The verb is in the perfect tense, which refers to an action in the past that has continuing results into the future. Peter is saying that the giving has already been done. It is not something we have to wait for. As a result of the redemptive work of Christ, everything we need has been placed in our storehouse. When he says "everything," what exactly does Peter mean? He tells us. We have everything that we need for "life and godliness." Peter is not only saying that God has provided all we need for eternal life but for godliness as well. What does he mean by godliness? He means a God-honoring life from the time I am accepted into God's family until the time I go to be with him in eternity. We have been given everything we need to think, desire, and behave in a godly way in the situations and relationships in which God has placed us! What an awesome provision!
- Peter tells us the purpose of this great provision. It is not so that we would be personally happy (nice job, marriage, family, church, neighborhood, vacations, retirement, etc.). No, God's

purpose is that we would become participants in his divine nature! God's ultimate purpose is not personal happiness but personal holiness. God is addressing my most significant need, which is not external or emotional but moral. It is a heart ruled by the Lord rather than by "evil desires." If my heart is ruled by evil desires, I will participate in the "corruption in the world" rather than in the work of Christ. I will not have a harvest of good fruit. Peter is saying that the most significant thing that God saves us from is us! Because of his abundant supply, we no longer have to live "unto ourselves," but for "him who died for us and was raised again" (2 Corinthians 5:15).

- Finally, Peter tells us what will happen when we start living out our identity in Christ (vv. 5–8). It will change the way we live. We will not settle for a little bit of Christian character. We will want all that God has provided. We will see the relationships and situations of daily life as opportunities to get in increasing measure what belongs to us in Christ. If we understand our identity, we will have a progressive growth paradigm for life. We will not look at life as a minefield. We will not live to avoid, escape, or defend. We will live with hope, expectancy, and courage. We will live as one who is rich, not poor.

As people begin to apply the new insights they have been given and the new commitments they have made, this is the identity they need. They will tend to forget who they are. (Moses: "Who am I, that I should go?" Gideon: "But Lord, how can I save Israel? My clan is the weakest . . . and I am the least in my family.") They need to be reminded of their position (children of God) and their resources (everything they need) over and over again.

4. Providing Accountability

As change is applied to daily living, the Bible gives us two things to remember. First, as we help restore a person to where God wants him to be, we should "carry each other's burdens" (Galatians 6:2). We are also told that we should "encourage one another daily" (Hebrews 3:13). These passages have much to offer us as we think about accountability.

- Accountability is not about being a private detective.
- It is not about trying to do the work of the Holy Spirit.
- It is not about being someone's conscience.
- It is not about forcing someone to obey.
- It is not about chasing someone who is running or looking for someone who is hiding.

Accountability is about providing loving structure, guidance, assistance, encouragement, and warning to a person who is fully committed to the change God is working in his life. Let's look at these five elements of accountability.

1. *Accountability provides structure.* Life is often messy and chaotic. Change seems easier when being discussed than it does when being applied to life. Accountability provides an outside system of structure ("Do these things during this period of time") that can be immensely helpful to the person attempting something for the first time.

2. *Accountability provides guidance.* Often a person will want to do what is right but won't be sure how to do it. At these times it is a great benefit to have someone standing alongside to provide ongoing wisdom as to the "where," "when," and "how" of change.

3. *Accountability provides assistance.* There are times when the person is not able to make the needed changes alone (example: a difficult talk with a wife, friend, child) and he literally needs someone there with him, helping him make the changes that are needed.

4. *Accountability provides encouragement.* Change is difficult and people get beaten down. They are tempted to question their commitments or even to quit. In these times, they need someone they trust alongside them, who knows their situation and who can encourage them to continue.

5. *Accountability provides warning.* There are times when people confess the need for change, but then begin to rebel against it when they realize the cost and work involved. These people need to be warned of the consequences that their disobedience and rebellion will bring. They need to be reminded that they will harvest what they have sown (Galatians 6:7).

Accountability is not about chasing a person who does not want to change or trying to do the work of the Holy Spirit. It is the willingness to provide ongoing help to the person who is fully committed to the "put off/put on" process.

There are three questions to ask as you seek to provide ongoing accountability.

1. What kinds of ongoing help will this person need?
2. How often will I need to be in contact with him for change to continue?
3. Are there other resources in the Body of Christ that would be helpful during this period of change? How can I connect this person to those resources?

Remember, as the person begins to apply new insights and new commitments to his situations and relationships, it is important to remind him of his identity in Christ and to provide ongoing accountability.

THE BIG QUESTION: Do you help others bear the burden of change by providing biblical accountability and affirming their identity in Christ?

CPR

Concepts

1. Human beings always live out of some sense of identity.

2. Every believer needs to understand his union with Christ.

3. In times of change, each of us needs loving accountability.

Personalized

1. Do I look at myself and my life from the perspective of who I am in Christ?

2. Does a daily recognition of my identity in Christ shape the way I think, speak, and act?

3. Do I humbly seek and receive accountability as God calls me to change?

Related to others

1. Do I look for opportunities to remind others of their identity in Christ?

2. Do I look for where and how I can help others bear the load of change?

3. Am I willing to provide loving accountability to others as they apply new insights and commitments to their daily lives?

Make It Real

Consider your Personal Ministry Opportunity using the following questions.

1. What kind of accountability do you need to supply so that change and growth will continue to take place?

2. Where has this person (group) tended to forget who he is in Christ? What Scripture passages could you use to encourage a clear sense of this identity?

3. Describe how you would use one of these passages with the person.

4. Look back over your work on your Personal Ministry Opportunity and list some of the specific things you have learned about being an instrument of change in God's redemptive hands.

5. What prayer requests do you have for the person you have sought to serve? What prayer requests do you have for yourself?

At a Glance

4 **Following
the Wonderful Counselor
in personal ministry**

2 Corinthians 5:14–20

3 *Understanding your heart struggle.*

James 4:1–10

5/6 **Love**

John 13:34

**Building relationships
in which God's work will thrive**

2

*What rules
the heart
will shape
and direct
the behavior.*
Ezekiel 14:1–5

7/8 **Know**

Hebrews 4:14–16

**Getting to know people,
discovering where change is needed**

9/10 **Speak**

Proverbs 20:5

Speaking the truth in love

1 *Three Questions Everyone Asks:*
1. Why do people do the things they do?
2. How does lasting change take place?
3. How can I be an instrument of change in the life of another?

11/12 **Do**

Galatians 6:1–2

Applying change to everyday life

FIRM FOUNDATION
Creation—Fall—Redemption
Genesis 1 • Genesis 3 • Hebrews 3:12–13

Each one needing help; each one called to be a helper.